PRAISE FOR *THE BUSINESS ANALYSIS HANDBOOK*

'If you are contemplating joining or are new to the profession, then you will benefit from the practical guidance contained in *The Business Analysis Handbook*. The author recognizes and emphasises that an effective business analyst needs a mixture of both technical and sociological skills. Highlights include identification of the main challenges of the business analysis profession, recognition of how modalities help the business analyst to plan the most effective way of working with people and an overview of the most common process and data modelling techniques.

'If you read this book from cover to cover you will get a clear picture of what business analysis is all about and what is expected of a business analyst. Equally you would do well to use the book as a reference to guide and inspire you in doing your everyday work.'
Suzanne Robertson, Principal and Founder of The Atlantic Systems Guild

'What makes this book unique from others is its no-nonsense approach to explaining key business analysis concepts, which are brought to life by the author's personal experiences. Whether you are new to business analysis or an experienced practitioner, *The Business Analysis Handbook* is an essential reference guide for your book collection.'
Pardeep Dhanda, Communities Director, IIBA UK

'*The Business Analysis Handbook* will meet a genuine need amongst business analysts for clear, practical advice on many issues that they commonly come across in their work, which aren't all discussed in the more formal literature. If you're starting out on a business analysis career, I strongly recommend you read this book.'
Nick de Voil, President, IIBA UK

'Helen Winter's book provides a good overview of the business analysis role, processes, techniques, and deliverables. It is written such that it is valuable to both someone wanting to enter the business analyst role, and experienced business analysts looking for a thorough overview. It covers both hard and soft skills required for a business analyst, and addresses some of the challenges you will face as a business analyst, along with tips to overcome those challenges. The book also provides some valuable templates to help you get started. Overall, *The Business Analysis Handbook* is a well-rounded book for business analysts.'
Vicki McCracken, former Requirements Analyst and author of *Requirements for an MDM Solution*

'This book draws on Helen Winter's extensive experience as a leading business analyst. Recognizing the value of effective communications, the author offers insights into communication techniques, encompassing verbal, visual and written styles for different audiences and scenarios. She combines clarity of style with wry observations drawn from real life to bring the subject alive, delivering insight, communications and guidance for managing different situations and stakeholders in a well-structured, genuinely readable text.'
Alistair Roberts, Chief Technology Officer

'I had the pleasure to work with Helen Winter on a very challenging digital transformation programme, where we collaborated on shaping the emerging practices, and her experience helped us all to keep the focus on outcomes. It was very inspiring to observe how Helen used her drive and vast experience to establish good BA practices in a wider business, and effectively design training programmes for her team, as well as iteratively improving practices in the agile delivery context. I am really looking forward to having this great reference on my bookshelf!'
Susan Engel, Lead Product and Innovation Consultant, Zuhlke Engineering

'Helen Winter's book is a great demonstration of her knowledge of business analysis. It is a great aid for business analysts wanting to refer to techniques to help support them with current projects, tasks and people interested in the profession. Having had the pleasure of working with the author it's great to see the final results and now more people will be able to benefit from her wisdom.'
Leanne Carnegie, Business Analyst

'Helen Winter has produced an insightful and engaging addition to the published body of work on business analysis. This is a must-read book for anybody considering a career in the profession or for practicing business analysts across all levels of experience.'
Marc Edwards, Business analyst

'Helen Winter demonstrates in clear language the value of and need for the business analyst role. She shows how techniques can be applied to enable business change in a pragmatic manner by highlighting the importance of the business analyst in being an informed and trusted partner. *The Business Analysis Handbook* is the essential A to Z for both budding and experienced business analysts, which provides an invaluable balance of theory and application.'
Richard Snow, Head of Change

'So many people are "doing" business analysis without even realising it, and certainly without formal training or recognition. This superbly organised book demystifies the subject, and serves as a valuable primer for anyone considering a career in the field or interested in applying its principles to their work: in a world where change and uncertainty are the new normal, embedding business analysis throughout the organisation leads to higher quality thinking, which in turn leads to better decision making. The section providing tools and templates will be especially welcomed by anyone wishing to understand and emulate best practice.'
Alison Jones, Innovation Strategist, host of the Extraordinary Business Book Club and founder of Practical Inspiration Publishing

'This book is amazing, and I vouch that the techniques presented in this book are practical, as I have seen Helen Winter deliver successful business change programmes using the techniques that she has shared in this book. I have recommended that all my staff read this book, as I truly believe that following the principles contained in it will help them build a stronger trust with the customer and deliver solutions to their expectations.'
Anil Passi, Director, Fusion Practices

'Helen Winter is committed to growing her business analysis expertise (the profession has to grow to remain useful). This book is her gift to the business analyst community to help others do the same.'
Alex Papworth, Adventurer

The Business Analysis Handbook

Techniques and questions to deliver better business outcomes

Helen Winter

KoganPage

Publisher's note
Every possible effort has been made to ensure that the information contained in this book is accurate at the time of going to press, and the publishers and author cannot accept responsibility for any errors or omissions, however caused. No responsibility for loss or damage occasioned to any person acting, or refraining from action, as a result of the material in this publication can be accepted by the editor, the publisher or the author.

First published in Great Britain and the United States in 2019 by Kogan Page Limited

2nd Floor, 45 Gee Street
London
EC1V 3RS
United Kingdom

122 W 27th St, 10th Floor
New York, NY 10001
USA

4737/23 Ansari Road
Daryaganj
New Delhi 110002
India

www.koganpage.com

© Helen Winter, 2019

ISBNs

Hardback   978 1 78966 023 4
Paperback   978 0 7494 9706 4
Ebook   978 0 7494 9705 7

British Library Cataloguing-in-Publication Data

A CIP record for this book is available from the British Library.

Library of Congress Cataloging-in-Publication Data

Names: Winter, Helen (Business analyst), author.
Title: The business analysis handbook : techniques and questions to deliver
    better business outcomes / Helen Winter.
Description: London ; New York, NY : Kogan Page, 2019. | Includes
    bibliographical references and index.
Identifiers: LCCN 2019022467 (print) | LCCN 2019022468 (ebook) | ISBN
    9781789660234 (hardback) | ISBN 9780749497064 (paperback) | ISBN
    9780749497057 (ebook)
Subjects: LCSH: Business analysts.
Classification: LCC HD69.B87 W56 2019 (print) | LCC HD69.B87 (ebook) |
    DDC 658–dc23
LC record available at https://lccn.loc.gov/2019022467
LC ebook record available at https://lccn.loc.gov/2019022468

Typeset by Integra Software Services, Pondicherry
Print production managed by Jellyfish
Printed and bound by CPI Group (UK) Ltd, Croydon, CR0 4YY

CONTENTS

LIST OF FIGURES AND TABLES

TABLES

ABOUT THE AUTHOR

Helen Winter owns a consultancy business helping organizations to understand the root causes of their problems, their requirements and how to turn them into solutions. She has over 20 years' business change experience, having worked as a consultant on all stages of the project lifecycle on large-scale transformation programmes within the financial services, regulation, insurance and utilities sectors.

Helen has been sharing her knowledge and experience for a number of years on a blog she founded called businessbullet.co.uk. This promotes business change and business analysis as well as providing practical methods for overcoming typical problems that occur in the profession.

Helen's hobbies include running, and she has run two full marathons. She has an interest in psychology and has gained a qualification in hypno-psychology.

If you would like to know more after reading this book there are lots of articles you can read on businessbullet.co.uk, or you can get in touch with Helen directly through the businessbullet.co.uk website.

ACKNOWLEDGEMENTS

Thank you to my late father, who always encouraged me to give things a go and gave me my sense of adventure. He wasn't around to see me write this book but used to read every article I wrote on businessbullet.co.uk and gave words of encouragement. Also, thank you to my mum, who made sure that my book was mum proofed. I believe that what I write should always be understandable to a complete beginner, and I loved it when she started to explain when a company should and shouldn't use agile on a night out together. I nearly spilled my drink all over myself. Thanks to my husband, Jon Winter, who has had to put up with me writing this book at every spare opportunity in between work, walking the dog and sleeping.

Thanks to Penny Pullan, who has been a huge inspiration. She recommended I write a book and put me in touch with Alison Jones. Alison provides coaching on writing business book proposals and really helped me pull my thoughts together on what I wanted to achieve.

Thanks to Amy Minshull and Adam Cox at Kogan Page for being so supportive and being on hand for advice and feedback.

A huge thank you to Leanne Carnegie, Marc Edwards and Aurvinder Dhanda for being beta readers for parts of the book and providing their feedback. Also, thanks to Jack Lees-Manning, Julie Bott, Saemma Khwaja and Matt Silvester for their emotional support when I was writing the book.

01

Preparation for business analysis

Introduction

Business analysis (BA) has evolved over time to cover a wide subject area. It is a broad concept, and the scope of its application can be hard to define to people outside of the profession. It is still relatively new to some industries. There isn't a dedicated business analysis qualification at universities, so some people might not even be aware of it as a career.

Some people will find after reading this chapter that they are already performing some of the functions of a business analyst; others might realize they have the skills to succeed in this role. In this chapter I will outline my journey, along with **techniques and questions to deliver better business outcomes** to help you understand business analysis and be the best business analyst.

You will get an understanding of why business analysis is important, as causes of project failure often can be remediated by good business analysis such as understanding the customer's problems and requirements and ensuring this is carried through for all stages of the change taking place.

There is more than one approach for dealing with change in projects. There is much talk about companies moving to agile, but it might not always be appropriate, as there are differences in circumstances. This chapter will enable you to understand what waterfall and agile are and when they are appropriate.

I've then concluded this chapter with typical challenges found in business analysis. It can be a fulfilling career but is not suited to everyone. Therefore, it is important for anyone considering a career in it to be aware of the challenges they will face.

Questions covered in this chapter about preparing
for business analysis

This chapter answers the following questions:

- What is business analysis?
- How did I become a business analyst?
- What are some tips on becoming a business analyst?
- What skills are needed for business analysis?
- What are the reasons for having business analysis?
- What are the different project methodologies and when is it best to use each one?
- What are the different types of roles in business analysis?
- What are the different business analysis artefacts?
- What are the main challenges facing someone who does business analysis?

What is business analysis?

Business analysis helps in defining the scope, quality and completeness of solutions to implement change in a business whilst meeting the business's needs. It is about being able to use techniques to identify the right questions to ask to maintain the vision of the business, and to identify the problems to be resolved, the business requirements and the solution requirements. It ensures all of these are understood between all the stakeholders involved and that they are documented. Business requirements set out what the business wants. Solution requirements show how each of the business requirements can be met. This provides a lower level of detail so that whoever takes the solution forward knows how to make it happen. Many tools and techniques have been developed over the last 20 years not only so we can understand what questions should be asked but also to help remove ambiguity, uncover missing information and ensure a common understanding.

In an IT context, business analysis provides guidance to developers for developing solutions and helps architects select the right set of systems and toolsets to meet business requirements. It is important to remember that not all requirements need an IT solution, and it is just as important for business analysis to include defining business solutions. This may involve helping the business define how it is going to meet requirements and assessing the impact. Examples of business solutions could be new business processes, changes to documentation and changes to a target operating model.

These days a lot of cloud products are selected off the shelf. Therefore business analysis work also helps in finding the right off the shelf solutions and feeds into the procurement process.

Business analysis can involve the sourcing of information required to make decisions by observation and collecting metrics to prove or disprove hypotheses before they become a project. See Chapter 3 for more detail on the techniques to ensure a project will solve the right problem and that it is worth doing.

Business analysis provides a structure for being able to provide traceability from the solution to the requirements and vision, knowing what to test and measuring whether the solution was successful and whether the benefits expected were met.

Its outputs can be reused longer-term to enable the business to have the knowledge to incorporate the solutions as usual practices and for similar future projects. The impact is that any future changes to the solution can be incorporated faster, because the thinking, processes, business rules and quality of the solution are documented in some form and readily accessible. It can be very expensive for example to pay an IT developer to work out what a system does by looking at the code and working it out. Having how the system works available in a format that can be understood by a wider audience will provide less reliance on technical expertise later. This is applicable when modifying an existing system, as opposed to a greenfield project implementation where the source code does not yet exist.

How did I become a business analyst?

My journey to becoming a business analyst started when I chose to do a business information technology degree at Staffordshire University in the UK. The technical and business skills along with the experience I gained on this course allowed me to get my first job as a consultant at a major consultancy. This job involved a mixture of business analysis, system analysis, development and configuration of the company's business intelligence software. I loved going into different industries and understanding their different reporting needs.

After this, I worked as a developer at the financial regulator, but missed the interaction with the stakeholders from my previous role. I was fortunate though to find mentorship there from a business analyst, obtained additional qualifications in the form of the International Diploma in Business Analysis certified by the British Computing Society and worked my way to becoming a business analyst.

Working at the financial regulator gave me lots of experience working on very large and complex projects, because their projects often had to account for all financial companies. This is where I picked up many structured techniques to ensure that all scenarios are identified to cater for each of the circumstances different-sized companies and ways of working bring. Examples of techniques used were context diagrams, process modelling and use cases.

Eventually I took a business analyst job at a utilities company. The biggest lesson I learnt with utilities was around putting together business cases and business transformation.

After a few years I got a job working in Birmingham city centre back in finance. You might be interested to know that the manager who hired me said that she specifically liked the fact that I had worked in an unrelated industry because it proved I had cross-transferable skills.

My next career move was to an insurance company. I was responsible at one point for leading 12 business analysts on a customer services transformation project. I also moved into the business architecture team for a while before deciding to move back into the business analysis team to lead on a large actuarial change programme. This is why I have lots of tips in later chapters for overcoming technical jargon.

I then decided to set up my own consultancy company. I got to utilize my skills with facilitating workshops, estimating and scoping, contributing business cases, process modelling, requirements gathering, utilizing data warehousing knowledge and logical data modelling, among others. I also got to expand on skills such as target operating models and creating knowledge handover frameworks.

I also set up a blog that I called businessbullet.co.uk to help other business analysts or those interested in business analysis. This has become very popular, and I've been able to help a number of people over the years. It also helped me to understand and remember the lessons I had learnt, as it meant having to analyse and articulate what went well and what to avoid.

What are some tips on becoming a business analyst?

Here are some tips based on what I have learnt throughout the journey in my career based on how I have done it and how I have mentored others. This is applicable for both a career change and a first step into the world of work.

Trainee positions/related roles

If you are not in work there are many opportunities to find jobs that can act as a stepping stone to business analysis, jobs that already include business analysis or even jobs that are trainee junior positions. There are many companies that are willing to recruit junior business analysts and provide them with coaching and training. The benefit to the companies is that they get to mould their recruits in the way that suits them best. For these positions they are looking for people with a willingness to learn, an aptitude to get on with others and confidence. My first job was as a consultant, and that included having to do business analysis as part of my role.

Volunteering and shadowing

If you are working and aren't currently involved in business analysis, the best way to get involved is to make yourself known and volunteer to shadow other business analysts if possible. Shadowing others may also allow you to carry out some BA tasks with a business analyst's guidance and supervision if you can build trust and rapport with the business analyst. If you can do this, read up about some of the techniques business analysts use and, if you get to try them out, make sure you ask for feedback. Identify opportunities to run your own small project to identify improvements and make use of modelling processes. It is very rare for people to say no if you offer to help. Another idea is to offer to help minute a meeting, watch how the facilitator does it and as you build confidence up volunteer to help organize or run a meeting. There are tips on running meetings and how to avoid some of the most common pitfalls in Chapter 2.

Researching business analysis

Find out as much as you can about business analysis. It covers a wide area, and it may be the case that you will want to focus on a particular area of it. This chapter will give you a good overview as to the breadth of business analysis and the type of roles within it.

Making your intentions clear

If you work for a company that has a business analysis team, make sure you let your manager know that you are looking for opportunities to get exposure to business analysis and arrange to chat to the business analyst manager. Both may be able to make recommendations to you of courses to go on and may be able to arrange for you to have some involvement in business analysis. They may also be able to arrange a secondment, which is a fixed period for being part of the team to try it out. When the secondment ends you may have to go back to your old job but then at least you have experience you can demonstrate when a permanent position comes up. If you get the opportunity to do a secondment make sure you ask for written feedback from the people you work with not just for your own development but also to show proof of your capabilities and experience.

Qualifications

There are two main professional bodies related to evidencing capability in business analysis. These are the British Computing Society (BCS) and the International Institute of Business Analysis (IIBA). You will need to work out which qualification route to take. You only need to do one. I cannot emphasize enough how important it is to learn about the techniques and tools available, and both qualifications provided by these associations will provide good coverage. You may be able to put together a business case for your company paying for some of the courses, as business analysis covers a wide area and still may be suitable for your current role. I was able to put a business case together at my company to gain the BCS qualification before obtaining the role of business analyst.

Project work exposure

See whether you can get involved with project work to give yourself some exposure to it. Project work by its very nature only lasts for the duration of the project. Depending upon the size of the project it may only be part time and could last for a couple of months to at most a couple of years. The reason I mention this is because the implications are that the different projects by their very nature will entail different people, different environments and continual learning. This doesn't suit some people, and I have mentored trainees who have decided that business analysis isn't for them because of these factors.

Cross-transferable skills

Remember that you may already have some cross-transferable skills such as communication, meeting facilitation, process mapping, problem solving or presenting. You don't have to have the job title 'business analyst' to do business analysis. There is often business analysis involved in many roles. By reading what business analysis is and the skills required you may see correlations with what you already do. When you start getting experience then write about it to confirm your knowledge and market it to others. See whether you can get a mentor, and consider joining a professional association, which will also be able to provide you with guidance.

What skills are needed for business analysis?

Listening and communication

Communication is a key skill, as business analysis involves listening and talking to different stakeholders at different levels, gaining consensus with different parties who may have very different points of view and being able to challenge them to prioritize when all requirements cannot be mandatory. There will be times when you must contact people you haven't met before and with varying levels of seniority. Your communication skills must be good enough to cope with doing this. This can feel difficult in the early stages, but there are techniques that can help. For example, you could set up an introductory informal chat about who you are and what you are doing and to find out from them what they hope you can help them with.

Likeability

Likeability and relationship management are important. You need to be able to get people to want to help you, as you will need them to do things for you but have no management authority. Stakeholders may not understand the level of detail you need from them or why they should provide you with some of the information needed. If they like you, they are more likely to give you the opportunity to explain to them. Make efforts to get to know and show an interest in them to build rapport. I will always remember on one of my first projects the business stakeholders saying to me that they would not give me their requirements because IT projects never delivered what they wanted. I had to build their trust and find ways to build rapport with them. There happened to be a spare desk in their area. I decided to sit in it and offered to map their processes for them to help new members of their team. This led them to thinking of me as one of them and enabled me to gain their trust. I was then able to progress the project, which did end up as a success.

Tenacity

Typical challenges that need tenacity are working out where to start, getting stakeholders' time, keeping everyone's attention and focus in workshops, persuading stakeholders to part with information they may not want to give or see the point of providing, overcoming ambiguity, and chasing sign-offs of documentation, among others. If an organization or people you deal with in it are new to business analysis there might not be an understanding of the value you will add until you have demonstrated it.

Adaptability

Adaptability is vital, as not all stakeholders will think in the same way, and they will have different behaviours and beliefs. It's important therefore to be able to adapt to different approaches to suit your audience and situation. There are also so many different tools and techniques that can be used to suit different situations. Being able to use several of these will be beneficial.

Meeting facilitation

Meeting facilitation is a skill that can be improved with experience and by following the techniques explained in Chapter 2. Running meetings and workshops is a common method for eliciting requirements, understanding processes and discussing problems. It is important to know what you want to get out of a meeting, ensure the attendees understand what is expected of them and be able to achieve what you set out to do. This is difficult, because attendees may for example have their own agendas they want to cover, not agree with each other, not contribute, or go off on a tangent.

Techniques and documentation

The ability to apply techniques and write things down is essential. It is no good being great at eliciting requirements if you are unable to document what has been agreed, make it easy to understand and ensure it contains enough detail. It is very easy for everyone to think they are on the same page, but seeing the requirements on paper can make a huge difference. There are many diagram techniques such as mind maps, use case models, process diagrams and activity diagrams that can provide detail without generating huge amounts of narrative. In the past, requirements documents were big thick documents that it was difficult to get stakeholders to read. Diagrams are a fantastic way of documenting, because they take up far fewer pages, are unambiguous and are faster to produce.

Problem solving

Problem solving is another great skill, because it is important in business analysis to be able to identify, communicate and solve complex problems. The issues need to be communicated as well as the options and recommendations for resolving the problems.

What are the reasons for having business analysis?

There are several common factors that can be attributed to failing projects. These are all problems where business analysis done well can make a difference:

- poor stakeholder communication, for example between IT and the business;
- lack of engagement from the business;
- moving the problem elsewhere;
- not solving the problem or realizing the opportunity;
- poor requirements management;
- lack of clarity in the success criteria, including the objectives and completion requirements.

There are six main areas I will go through in turn to help prevent the problems mentioned above.

Stakeholder communication

Poor communication between IT and the business was the primary reason for the business analyst role becoming popular in the 1980s and 1990s. Business analysts were used to bridge the gap between IT and the business. The people in these roles tended to have an IT background so understood the level of detail these types of solutions required and were able to help the business understand. This remains a key benefit of business analysis. Business stakeholders will not necessarily be aware of the level of information required in IT solutions.

I will never forget key stakeholders telling me their business department had provided all of the requirements and no more interaction was needed. I gave them a list of questions and asked whether they had provided answers to them. Straight away they realized they hadn't provided these and understood why more involvement from them was necessary.

Projects tend to involve many different stakeholders across various sections of the business. Business analysts will be responsible for ensuring they have included all the relevant people to gather the big picture directly from individuals in these areas. It is easier to ensure a consensus on requirements if all the stakeholders are identified early on. Each set of stakeholders may have different perspectives and experiences impacting what they want in a solution. Getting this right at the beginning will save time.

Lack of engagement from the business

Business analysts can act as a voice for the business, making sure they engage when they need to and know enough to act on the business's behalf if required. As explained in the previous subsection, stakeholder communication is also key. It is the responsibility of the project manager to gain permission for the resources' time. However, it is still part of the business analysis role to engage the business and escalate where necessary if it is difficult to get people's time. Chapter 2 in this book provides a whole section on building effective working relationships to help with improving business engagement.

Moving the problem elsewhere

This is where solution evaluation, impact analysis and traceability are important. Solutions often get suggested to meet the business needs, but analysis is required to check the impact and to check it still meets the success criteria.

Not solving the problem or realizing the opportunity

The basis of a project will be a hypothesis about a perceived problem or opportunity. Problems can be very complex with possibly several causes and solutions. Business analysis involves investigating and confirming the hypothesis to ensure the right problem is being resolved and it is worth doing.

Poor requirements management

Business analysis is also about managing the requirements to ensure they are feasible, fit into the scope of the project and are of value to the business. Just because a requirement is stated doesn't mean that it should automatically be included. With requirements, lots of ideas get raised at the beginning, but these need to be challenged to ensure they are worth doing. A project is in danger of never being delivered if the scope is too large, there is no priority set for what to do first or there is no way of assessing impact and managing change.

Success criteria

Without success criteria there can be a lack of agreement on when a project is completed and whether it has been successful. Business analysis involves defining success criteria to ensure the quality of the solution will fit with the business needs.

What are the different project methodologies and when is best to use each one?

There are two main types of project methodologies: waterfall and agile. Which of these to use, and when, is very important. They manage the constraints of time, cost and scope in different ways.

Waterfall

The waterfall methodology involves defining requirements before design starts, then design being completed before development starts, and the process continuing sequentially. Each stage of the project is signed off before moving to the next one.

The rationale is that uncovering changes in the later stages will have a bigger impact on cost. Therefore, in theory, this methodology will require less rework, because the assumption is that stages are defined and completed as outlined, so do not then need to be repeated. If there are changes, these will be impact-assessed separately. The emphasis is very much on controlling the project by fixing the scope, because this is fixed at each sign-off stage.

There is more governance, as waterfall will ensure each stage is complete before moving on to the next, with documentation to match. This gives additional visibility for senior managers and checkpoints to how the project is progressing. This is useful for agreeing the budget at each successive stage as more is known about the project. The waterfall approach has been around for a fairly long period and is often seen as the easiest way to manage large complex projects.

Waterfall methodologies can be difficult to time-manage, as any delay to one stage will have a knock-on impact on the next. It is also criticized for being very rigid, because if there are lots of changes to the requirements after they are signed off then managing the changes separately may mean a slowness to react to them and the continuation of delivering something that has become out of date. In addition, not seeing the results until the very end may lead to changes that could have been dealt with sooner. It can encourage behaviours that can lead to projects failing if there is pressure to cut short the requirements so that it feels as though progress is being made. There can be a perception that a project isn't progressing unless people are working on delivery. It can then also squeeze testing at the end if the project has overrun, which can then lead to more quality flaws.

Agile

Agile works on a set of principles set out in 2001 known as the Agile Manifesto or formally the Manifesto for Agile Software (http://agilemanifesto.org/). This was produced by a group of developers who call themselves the Agile Alliance. The principles are:

- Individuals and interactions are more beneficial than processes and tools.
- Working software is more useful than comprehensive documentation.
- Customer collaboration is better than contract negotiation.
- Responding to change is more important than following a plan.

Processes and tools, comprehensive documentation, contract negotiation and following a plan are still desirable, but individuals and interaction, working software, customer collaboration and responding to change are considered more important.

The different stages of the project are broken down into chunks and worked on iteratively and incrementally. The requirements, design and development evolve rather than being all defined in sequential order. Another big difference is that the project teams all work together at the same time throughout the whole project, with an emphasis on daily contact and being self-organizing. Success is measured through the review of the end results rather than documentation. Improvements are made at the end of each iteration of work by the team reviewing what they have done and discussing how they can improve things.

The rationale in agile is that scope and requirements might change and breaking and delivering the work in smaller pieces will get the project delivered faster and enable continuous improvement by output being seen more quickly with the ability to make changes faster. The emphasis is very much on controlling the project by fixing time.

There is an even greater need for collaboration in an agile project, where a cross-section of people work together in a more intense way. If the project follows a scrum approach, there will be several meetings involving working as one team. Some of these will include daily stand-up meetings, refinement sessions to discuss requirements, sprint planning to plan how much work can be delivered in a time-boxed period, and sprint retrospectives to understand what lessons can be learnt. The concept of T-shaped teams is often prevalent, where all members of the team are expected to help each other out. They may have a narrow section of skills they use for their own role but will also have a much wider knowledge of other skills that are shared across the team.

There is a saying: 'Fail fast.' The idea behind it is that getting feedback more quickly will allow for a better product in the end because we can then learn quickly from our mistakes. To achieve this there must be collaborative working with close communication. Work output is delivered faster in smaller incremental chunks, so feedback and reflection for improvements need to be shared so the team can self-organize and make improvements if necessary.

The most valuable requirements are delivered to working software faster with continuous delivery. The advantage to this is quicker delivery to market and the ability to respond to change.

'Agile' is an umbrella term for several different types of agile methodologies, as it doesn't describe how to work to the principles described. Examples of some of the most common agile methodologies are scrum, Kanban, extreme programming and unified process (UP).

The disadvantages of agile approaches are that they tend to be very resource-intensive, as the developers and testers need to be involved sooner and there is much more involvement required of the customer stakeholders. Some organizations have handled this by reorganizing their corporate structure around product teams rather than by discipline.

Agile was originally associated with software development. However, it can be applied and be valuable to other business areas. The idea of being able to respond faster to change, work more collaboratively with others and learn from mistakes faster can be very appealing. For example, in marketing, people can obtain and respond quickly to customer feedback and work in an agile way with sales and operations to test out new products and services to get them to market faster.

Factors to be considered when choosing which project methodology to use for a project

TIMESCALE
If time is an important factor then agile techniques can deliver work sooner, because they are iterative, have the ability to run work in parallel and provide more releases. Daily contact between all parties will also help remove any blockers more promptly and ensure the project is kept on track.

SIZE OF A PROJECT
For the size of a project, choosing a methodology depends on how easy it is to break the project down into chunks, especially if the project is large. If it is difficult to do this then agile can introduce the risk of not ever being able to fix the scope, and the project could then run on and on.

REQUIREMENT STABILITY
If requirements are expected to stay fairly static once defined, then the waterfall approach could be a good fit. If requirements are expected to have the potential for change because there are a lot of unknowns or because of a fast-paced industry or environment, then agile might be a better fit.

GEOGRAPHICAL TEAM LOCATIONS

If all the stakeholders and development teams are in one geographical location, then using agile will be easier than for dispersed locations. This is because agile approaches have daily meetings to establish progress, what needs doing each day and blockers. See also the next subsection, 'Stakeholder involvement', for other reasons.

STAKEHOLDER INVOLVEMENT

Agile approaches tend to be more resource-intensive and require all types of stakeholders at the same time. They tend to require a dedicated team of the customer(s), business analyst(s), developer(s) and tester(s) all working together from the early stages of the project. If these resources cannot be made available at the same time, then agile is less feasible. The waterfall approach means that resources only need to be made available at the relevant stages of the project, and these are set out over a longer timescale.

THE CORPORATE CULTURE

The culture in agile teams needs to be self-organizing, and the roles of power are slightly different. This will impact the corporate culture. Teams need to feel empowered to make decisions together and to develop T-shaped teams, where team members have knowledge of not just a few skills in-depth but also a cross-range of shallower skills. This makes it easier for team working and collaboration. Everyone in the team needs to be able to work in the same way to support and collaborate with the others.

DELIVERY AND CAPABILITY APPROACH OF THE ORGANIZATION

Agile relies on regular releases, because it requires work to be completed in small regular chunks. If this isn't possible in your organization, then this method will be harder to adapt.

DEDICATED FACILITIES

Using an agile approach requires dedicated work areas and facilities. There must be space for the stakeholders to get together regularly to collaborate. Often there are lots of sticky notes and wall space used for planning out the work and agreeing priorities. Whiteboards are often used to show the progress of the team. Collaboration tools are used to share information, provide comments, and allocate and track work. Audio-conferencing and video-conferencing may also be necessary for collaborating over geographical sites. If these types of facilities are not available then using an agile methodology will be less feasible.

THIRD PARTIES

Working with third parties can require different approaches. Agile means all stakeholders must work in that way. I have come across so many circumstances where a third party will only follow a waterfall approach. Considerations then include whether the benefits of agile will be realized in this situation. If the scope needs to be fixed and changes managed separately then some of the benefits will not be relevant. Also, if traditional waterfall deliverables are insisted upon then the project may start out agile and then change to waterfall, which then risks providing just the disadvantages of both agile and waterfall.

GOVERNANCE

Companies that have a governance set-up based on a traditional waterfall approach will need to make allowances if they are considering an agile approach. Agile will not be suitable for a governance structure that insists on staged gates that need to be signed off before moving to the next stage. In these circumstances, permission will need to be granted to be able to work in parallel and report back based on the delivery of iterations instead of based on a release plan.

The same will apply to the way requirements are documented. Rather than detailed business requirements and solution requirements documents, a product backlog will need to be created. This will not contain all requirements at once but will be refined continually to detail the requirements just in time for them to be developed based on the value they hold with the business.

The governance around decision making may also be different in agile compared to waterfall, as the teams need to be empowered to make their own decisions.

TRAINING AND COACHING

Training and coaching in agile are required to understand the philosophy and what tasks are required and why. For those who have had no experience of agile, the ways of working may seem very different. The roles and the positions of power are different, and there are only three recognized roles in approaches such as scrum. Therefore there needs to be some understanding of what these roles are, how the traditional roles fit with them and how they can be adapted. There are several new concepts, which will be covered later in this book, such as product backlog, minimum viable product, iterations, velocity, sprints and sprint backlog, to become familiar with and understand. There are several meetings that are adhered to as part of standard practice, so these also must be understood and recognized. Fortunately, *The Scrum Guide* by Ken Schwaber and Jeff Sutherland can be freely downloaded from http://www.scrumguides.org/, which makes it easy for people to understand and learn the concepts and some of the methods.

There are also lots of agile games that have been invented to create a fun way to teach others the agile philosophy. These are all games that can help teach the concepts and roles and encourage collaboration and team work.

Many companies already have a standard project methodology, which is generally set in stone. However, it is useful to have an insight into what factors may play a part, when to consider alternatives, and the risks and benefits each of the methodologies contributes.

What are the different types of roles in business analysis?

Business analysis is a wide area so quite often has roles specializing in different parts. This section takes each of the different roles and explains the most common differences. Bear in mind the descriptions below are generalizations so will vary from company to company. Some companies may separate out these roles, whilst other roles may be more blended.

Where business analysis roles are separated out, as described below, there will be a need for collaboration between the roles for the following main reasons:

- To ensure handover and common understanding.
- To ensure traceability. The IT requirements need to align with the stakeholder requirements and align with the business needs and organizational strategy.
- To manage change and impact assessments.

Business analyst (other job titles may include process analyst or requirements engineer)

A business analyst will tend to be in a department outside of IT and be the voice of the business. This involves making sure the business gets what it wants and will be able to live with the solution. Business analysts may be within a business area or in a change team. They will be involved with business process analysis, gathering and documenting stakeholder requirements. They will write the requirements so they are non-solution-specific. This means that, no matter what solution is applied, the business requirements will be the same.

Business analysts' outputs will involve running workshops and being key communicators in the project making, ensuring that all the requirements are agreed between business stakeholders and that IT stakeholders understand the requirements to be taken forward to the solution stage.

Business analysts may take solutions forward that are business-specific and have no IT involvement. This would involve helping the business document its business processes after the solution has been delivered, helping it prepare the solutions that it can implement on its own and being involved with business readiness tasks.

In terms of deliverables, business analysts will tend to be involved in producing business process models and business requirements documents to allow an understanding of a business's processes and requirements. They will tend not to have any systems access and not have much in-depth system knowledge.

Systems analyst (other job titles may include IT business analyst)

A systems analyst will be involved with taking the stakeholder requirements from the business analyst and determining the IT system requirements. Systems analysts will write the requirements at a lower level of detail.

From a functional perspective, these analysts will set out at a detailed level the activities the system needs to perform, and the interactions required between the user and the system. The content of any screens and the data required will be set out. Business rules will be considered to demonstrate circumstances where functionality, visibility or data vary according to circumstance.

From a non-functional perspective, systems analysts will identify the qualities the systems need to address, such as security or performance. They will either have knowledge about the systems or work with the developers to understand the capabilities of the system to be used or created.

In terms of deliverables they tend to be involved in putting together functional requirements and non-functional requirements documents.

Business systems analyst

This is a combination of the business analyst and systems analyst roles described above.

Product owner

A product owner manages what is known in agile as the 'product backlog'. See the 'Overview of methodologies and picking the right one' section above for further explanation if required, or the 'Agile projects' section in Chapter 6. In other contexts, the product owner is known as a business subject matter expert. The product backlog is a list of all the requirements related to the project. The product owner is accountable for continually updating this and ensuring that it is ordered to deliver the items of the highest value to the business first. The development team will develop based on the order of priority given in the backlog. The product owner's decision is final, and the backlog is always clearly visible to the whole project team to enable them to plan and estimate their work. The items in the product backlog will start out as headings and ideas, but by the time they are ready for development and at the top of the product backlog in terms of priority they will have been refined to provide the detail that the development team need. It is the product owner's responsibility to make sure the product backlog provides enough detail for the development team to work from.

Digital business analyst

A digital business analyst is often associated with agile projects, as digital media such as the web tend to lend themselves well to agile ways of working. This is because it is very easy to get prototypes quickly in front of the customer and to react swiftly to changes. The role of a business analyst isn't specifically mentioned in agile or in the approaches associated with it. However, there is a need for business analysis, so often a digital business analyst is part of the team. A digital business analyst will help the product owner document and refine the requirements in the product backlog and be a key player in the team to ensure common understanding and agreements for how the solution will need to work.

Digital business analysts will work closely with product owners to help them investigate and understand the requirements if necessary and be their voice with the developers at times when product owners cannot be available.

In terms of deliverables, they will produce business process models/ customer journey flows in discovery, refine user stories and acceptance criteria in the product backlog, and work with the other team members to produce wireframes and working prototypes to play back to the business. They will be the first, before the business users, to review the IT outputs to ensure quality against the acceptance criteria to aid business confidence.

Business architect (other job titles may include lead business analyst or principal business analyst)

A business architect will be involved at the enterprise level, identifying the blueprint for the organization. This will have the impact of allowing an understanding of the different solutions required to support the strategy and goals of the business. The business architectural role will involve checking high-level processes for how the organization is supported, checking whether the organizational structure is fit for purpose, reporting on the 'as is' resource capability, investigating whether customer and supplier interactions are adequate, and comparing tools and technology against the business goals, the information held within the organization, and the culture. Where there are gaps between what is current and what is needed to support the direction of the organization, the business architect will get involved with helping to define the changes required.

The business architect may also be involved earlier on in a project and be responsible for setting out the vision and help with building the business case for a project. This involves understanding the business needs and determining the solution options for taking the business forward from a strategic point of view.

To do this, business architects will work with the business to understand the problems, opportunities and needs. They will also look at the processes and where improvements can be made, not necessarily IT related. For example, strategic solutions may involve reviewing and changing the target operating model. Business architects will have knowledge or be able to work with other IT architects to identify what solutions should be adapted considering the capabilities of the organization and the future direction.

In terms of deliverables they will tend to be involved with developing and presenting business cases to senior management, pulling together blueprints of the organization, target operating models and solution options papers.

What are the different business analysis artefacts?

Every piece of work a business analyst is involved with should result in some form of artefact. An artefact in the context of business analysis is to help the business stakeholders and the other stakeholders involved have a common understanding of what change is required to meet the needs of the business and to make the change happen. This section sets out some of the most common artefacts, along with a brief description and some alternative names these might be known by.

Business analysis approach   This document sets out the business analysis involvement for the work concerned to set expectations, feed into a wider plan and gain agreement on the deliverables. For example, if a waterfall approach is going to be applied then it may list deliverables described later in this section, for example a business requirements document or a solution document. The deliverables should all be agreed in advance so they can be fed into the project manager's plan, which must also contain the amount of estimated effort required. If this doesn't fit with the project timeline then there may be a period of negotiation with the project manager to understand how to bring the time down or to alter the plan. It might be the case that additional resources are required. This document is important, because any problems impacting a deadline can be discussed earlier on when there is more time to do something about it. It will also ensure the business analyst knows what is expected of him or her and other stakeholders in return know what to expect. It should be done at the start of a project. The deliverables in it will be specific to business analysis.

Change request   A change request is a form to be filled out when a waterfall approach has been used and there are changes required after an artefact or stage has been signed off. The waterfall approach baselines each document and doesn't allow any further changes unless a change request is raised. It is filled out by the person requesting the change and is impact-assessed by the people who would be involved with making the change happen. There will need to be a change control process set up to manage the change requests. Changes need to be prioritized, documented, communicated and implemented if approved. This is covered in more detail in Chapter 7.

Vision document or business case or feasibility study   This document is set out before a change becomes a project to justify the benefits and estimate the costs to ensure it is feasible and worth doing. Throughout the project this document can be referenced back to ensure its findings still stand to allow the project to continue. It is an important document, because senior management will use it to agree whether the money is worth spending and will stop the project if they think there have been additional higher unexpected costs or fewer benefits than predicted. It will set out the direction of the project and ensure all the stakeholders have the same view. It will also clarify the scope of the work to ensure focus and to prevent scope creep. Throughout the project the document will be used to check back that the solution being progressed still meets what it set out to do. Chapter 3 provides more detail on what is involved with this stage of a project and the activities to generate this type of document.

Business process document   This sets out the business's 'as is' and 'to be' processes in order to understand the activities that the business carries out prior to a change and what the desired activities will be after a change. The 'as is' state can be analysed to identify problems and opportunities for change. It also provides an understanding of the processes end to end, as, if the process goes across teams, then the different teams may only know their part in the process. It is only by looking at the complete picture that analysis can be conducted on what improvements can be made. This artefact should always be completed and agreed prior to the business requirements document. This is because it helps in understanding the scope of the requirements and that all business requirements should relate to a process. More detail on this document and how to put one together is covered in Chapter 4.

Business requirements document   This contains a catalogue for all the business requirements from a stakeholder's point of view, a priority for each and a justification. It may also contain processes if a separate business process document hasn't been written. It will ensure a consensus and understanding of all the business requirements in scope for the project, as it will need to be signed off before progressing the project to the next stage of design. Chapter 5 provides more detail on eliciting and documenting business requirements.

Use case model or context diagram   This is more a technique that could sit within most of the other artefacts. However, I have called it out separately because it is so useful and could easily stand on its own. The technique consists of a use case model, which is a Unified Modeling Language (UML) tool (see http://www.omg.org/spec/UML), or a context diagram. It can be used at a business level to set out the goals of a project and who needs to be involved. It can also be used at a solution level to identify which systems are in scope, what goals they need to achieve and who or what other system interfaces need to connect to them. It is a powerful tool, because setting out the scope in this manner provides an indication of the project's size. It would be difficult to justify a project as small change if there are several goals and human or system interfaces. Having this set out visually makes the size and complexity of the project much more transparent. The different levels will be covered in Chapters 5 and 6.

Solution requirements document or functional requirements document or use cases or user stories or prototypes   These artefacts set out the solution requirements but will vary in their level of detail and format. They all have in common the purpose of ensuring that the solution requirements are understood and acceptable to the business and IT stakeholders. Solution requirements set out how the stakeholder requirements are going to be met. Chapter 6 will provide more detail on the differences between these formats and when they are used.

Non-functional requirements document   A non-functional requirement is a quality, constraint or behaviour that the system being built must meet. There are two types of non-functional requirements: global, which applies generically across the solution; and non-global, which can be related to a functional requirement. The non-global requirements are normally included in the business or solution requirements document. The global ones tend to be separated out into a dedicated non-functional requirements document. This is because they normally require a wider range of stakeholders and take longer to negotiate. These will be covered in more detail in Chapter 6.

Data requirements document   This document focuses on understanding data requirements and the relationships between the data. This involves several techniques such as entity relationship modelling and data dictionaries. It is necessary to have separate techniques for understanding data requirements to ensure not only that all the data requirements are elicited but that they can be used to uncover gaps in the functional requirements. The techniques are worth knowing regardless of whether this document is used, because they are also powerful techniques for ensuring a common consensus of the same terms and definitions. Chapter 6 will provide more detail.

Product backlog   This artefact relates to agile projects only. It evolves over time and lists all of the work that needs to be done to meet the requirements. Software such as Jira or VSTS tends to get used, because it will allow the list of work to be managed and tracked. It can also be configured to suit the project and can cater for the different levels of work as and when required. The product backlog may start off as high-level headings and be broken down into more detail as the project progresses. The normal method is to use a technique that breaks the backlog down into user stories. The order of the product backlog is maintained to work first on the highest-priority items that will deliver the most value to the users or customers of the product. Chapter 6 will provide more detail of examples.

Increment   This artefact is also specific to agile projects. It shows the outcome of what product backlog items are delivered and approved at the end of a sprint. A sprint is the period of time, normally either two weeks or four weeks, where work has been broken down and agreed. Agile is about getting working software delivered in small chunks to learn from it rather than solely relying on documentation. Chapter 6 will provide more detail of examples.

Sprint backlog   This artefact is specific to agile projects. It allows the development team to choose which user stories they think they can deliver from the product backlog within a sprint time period adhering to the priority order. They will then add the tasks they need to complete to deliver each of the user stories. They will also add estimates for each task and update the time they spend on them daily.

Request for proposal (RFP)/request for information (RFI)   The RFP or RFI is written when goods or services are required from an outside supplier where no products or expertise is currently available to meet the needs of the project within the company. The purpose of it is to specify the needs and allow other companies to bid for the work.

Evaluation scoring matrix   The evaluation scoring matrix is written in conjunction with the RFP. It agrees the success criteria to ensure the best vendor is selected, allow all scorers to follow the same success criteria and provide objectivity to the process.

Options paper   If problems are encountered the business analyst can write an options paper. The paper should be short and aimed at senior stakeholders. It should specify the problems encountered and the reasons. It should state what the potential options are to resolve the problem. Finally it should make a recommendation with reasons. This then allows problems and resolutions to be understood and agreed so the project can proceed.

Gap analysis document   This is used to assess any gaps between what is desired and what is current. This may be a gap analysis comparing processes or systems.

Traceability document   A traceability document may be used at several stages to ensure that what is being produced traces back to the requirements, the scope and the benefits and success criteria expected.

Test strategy/test scripts   These are normally tester deliverables, but there may be occasions when the business analyst will contribute to writing them, be a reviewer, carry out testing or help coordinate with other testers and business users. The purpose is to ensure that all of the different business scenarios will be met by the system being changed.

Training materials/new business processes   These are normally trainer deliverables. However, there may be occasions when the business analyst will document new business processes and ensure training manuals are kept up to date.

Handover documentation   If business analysts encounter several problems during the delivery process they may be best placed to put a handover document together for various parties to ensure that resolutions have been formally captured. This is particularly important if any new manual workarounds get introduced as a result.

What are the main challenges facing someone who does business analysis?

There are five main challenges in business analysis.

Challenge 1: Getting others to understand the amount of detail you need

There is a certain amount of detail required to be able to turn requirements into solutions, not just from a functional perspective but also from a quality perspective. It is not unusual for stakeholders to think they have provided all of the information you require without realizing more information is needed. This challenge can be overcome by using the techniques in this book. Taking our customers on a journey enables them to understand what information they need to provide and helps to get them on board with understanding how much of their time is required.

Challenge 2: Stakeholders not knowing their requirements

This may happen especially if they are doing something completely new they haven't done before. This is where techniques come in such as understanding their pain points, what they want to achieve and their business processes. These are often better starting points, because the business is more likely to know these. The outputs then help to identify and form requirements.

Challenge 3: Stakeholders not understanding your role

This may happen if business analysis is new to the organization or if there are no clear job descriptions and roles for business analysis. This is closely related to challenge 2. This is why I always recommend having some informal chats with your stakeholders at the early stages to introduce yourself and to explain how you can help. Gaining trust is very important, because your stakeholders have their own business as usual jobs to do and they will need to understand the value added if they are to give up their own time to speak to you.

Challenge 4: Communicating effectively and getting everyone to have the same understanding

Conversations are not good enough on their own. It is an important skill to be able to document what has been agreed in a way that is easy for others to understand. There are several techniques in this book for not only ensuring that everyone leaves a meeting with the same understanding but also on how to document. There are diagrams that can be used to show detail all on one page that would take up dozens of pages if written in narrative form.

Challenge 5: Stakeholders trying to bypass the process
and go straight to the solution

If stakeholders think they know the solution it can be even more difficult to understand the requirements behind it. You may be thinking 'Why does that matter?' It is because the solutions can change very easily depending upon time, scope and budget. There are almost always several ways to approach a solution and very rarely only one solution. Therefore it is important to understand the business requirements to enable traceability back for success and to enable flexibility if more than one solution needs to be investigated. The solution may change several times, so you don't want to keep rewriting the requirements each time.

02

Effective working relationships

Introduction

Building effective working relationships is an essential part of business analysis. Without the ability to collaborate with different roles and personalities in an organization, it would be difficult to obtain the information you need to be successful. Therefore, communication is key. It is important to understand the different types of stakeholders and how their expectations may vary. There are several techniques you can use to help build up an effective working relationship, and we will cover these. We will go through and explain the different approaches individuals take to communication and how people think in different ways. For example, they may go straight to the detail before explaining the context, or they may generalize or delete or distort information. This chapter will teach you how to recognize when these situations occur and how to respond.

Facilitating meetings is another important skill in business analysis, because it is an essential technique for eliciting requirements. Best practice tips will be provided to allow you to run your meetings effectively, which is crucial, as time can be limited with your stakeholders.

Questions covered in this chapter to help build effective relationships

This chapter answers the following questions:

- What types of stakeholders will you need to engage with?
- How do you build effective working relationships with your different stakeholders?
- How do you change your communication approach to meet the needs of your stakeholders?

- What do you do when stakeholders go straight to the solution without explaining the context or vision?
- Why is getting requirements/information from stakeholders so difficult and how do you overcome it?
- How do you run a workshop/meeting effectively?

What types of stakeholders will you need to engage with?

There is a mixture of different stakeholders you will need to engage with in business analysis. Often business analysts will act like the glue between all of the stakeholders to create joined-up thinking and a common understanding. This is not easy, as the stakeholder roles are very different, with different skillsets and often completely different personalities.

In addition, you aren't their manager, they might not understand the level of information you need from them and they might not even understand your role. It's therefore important to understand some techniques you can employ to make your life easier. These will equally apply to the other stakeholders mentioned.

The main stakeholders you are likely to encounter are:

- business stakeholders;
- project managers;
- architects (enterprise/solution);
- developers;
- testers;
- third parties.

Below I will outline considerations when working with these different stakeholders. I will explain how as a business analyst you can most effectively work alongside these parties. All the parties will have different perspectives, and an understanding of their job roles will give you a starting point in how their views differ. I also provide an overview of what their expectations may be of you, the difference between their role and yours, the overlaps and what potential challenges may need to be overcome.

Collaboration with business stakeholders

Business analysts represent business areas in a company to ensure their clients get solutions that meet their needs and are long lasting after the project is delivered. Therefore, it is important to work on building a rapport and to understand the expectations. Business stakeholders will have other work to do that competes for their time. The challenge for you will be to get enough time and information from them to be able to elicit, document and gain approval of the required standard and detail.

Collaboration with project managers

The project manager has the overall responsibility for a project. The project manager's focus is on its delivery within scope, budget and timescales and managing associated risks. A business analyst is involved to a lower level of detail supporting all the areas the project manager is responsible for. In comparison the business analyst focus is more on being the voice of the business, ensuring the solution maps back to the requirements and the business can live with the project solution once it is delivered. Where there are areas of overlap, these tend to be around setting out the vision, planning and stakeholder engagement.

The involvement of business analysts in pre-project work, setting out the vision and determining high-level business needs tends to vary by organization. Depending upon the organizational structure it can be led by the project manager, the business analyst or a mixture of both.

The project manager and business analyst both are involved with stakeholder engagement and often with the same set of stakeholders. This can often lead to one or the other not being involved in meetings that can affect them. It is therefore important for the business analyst and project manager to understand the difference in the information they receive so they can ensure the other party is involved where relevant. For instance, if stakeholders speak about business requirements to the project manager, they should ensure the stakeholder is asked to raise this with the business analyst. Likewise, if the stakeholders talk to the business analyst about project delivery timeframes then the business analyst should refer them to the project manager.

Another benefit of a good working relationship with the project manager that I have often found is that the business analyst will come across warning signs of issues well before anyone else. This is due to continuous involvement and regular contact with stakeholders. Good collaboration will enable discussions as to whether immediate action is required and an understanding of escalation at the appropriate points.

Collaboration with enterprise/solution architects

Business analysts must collaborate with enterprise architects (EA) and solution architects (SA) to help them select the right set of systems and toolsets to meet business requirements.

There are many types of artefacts that business analysts produce that will need to tie in with and influence the architecture. Problem statements, requirements, non-functional requirements, business processes, success criteria, wireframes and personas, among others, will all have an impact on what solutions will be suitable.

There are also some artefacts that require a combination of effort from both a business analyst and an architect. For example, an options paper setting out the issue, options and recommendations is one deliverable. A request for proposals setting out what is required to enable third parties to bid for work is another.

In the digital age, technology is even more important for driving strategy. Traditionally, understanding the business processes would help to determine the technology to be used to support them. Now a BA may need to rely on an EA/SA's expertise to understand what is possible when analysing requirements to overcome business problems or realize opportunities.

Collaboration with developers

Developers will need the most detail behind the requirements. They will want solution requirements that will remove ambiguity for them and make it clear what they need to do.

I've often found working closely with the developers through the design period is useful for discussing and drawing out options together. It then helps to guide the developers and ensure they understand the requirements and remove any 'gold plating'. Gold plating is when additional features are added over and above the requirements. It can be very tempting to include these if the developers believe it is easy for them to do so. However, there is a knock-on impact when it comes to testing, so it may not be as good an option as it first appears.

Collaboration with testers

Testers will need to plan their test strategy and build test scripts based on the requirements you write. They will also expect you to review their test strategy and test scripts. This is an important duty of business analysts, as it will be easier for you than for most of the other parties to spot any gaps.

Collaboration with third parties

If your company outsources any of its IT or buys out of the box solutions rather than using customized internal development, there is a strong chance you will have to deal with third party providers. How the relationship is set up will have a significant effect on the success of the project. You will need to build up a rapport, so the third parties know how and when to engage you. The ideal is for them to feel comfortable that you can help them resolve any issues with understanding requirements or will be able to help them obtain further information if necessary.

How do you build effective working relationships with your different stakeholders?

This sets out some of the key considerations for effective working relationships during a project or change. These are applicable to all the types of stakeholder relationships described previously.

Manager support and permission

Ideally the project manager or the stakeholder's manager will set the scene in advance with the stakeholders identified so they understand why you need to speak with them. If their time is planned in and they know their manager has given them permission to speak with you then it will be easier to get their time. If their manager has given them permission to speak with you then it will be easier to schedule in time.

Understanding of business analyst role

Ensuring the stakeholders understand how you will benefit them is important to the relationships to ensure they give you their time and provide you with the information you need. Not all business stakeholders have worked with a business analyst before, so don't assume they will automatically know. The business analyst's primary focus is to ensure that what is delivered is in line with the business needs so that at the end of the project the benefits are realized.

One option for how to do this could be in the form of a presentation to explain how you are going to help, the deliverables you will produce, how they will be used and what you need in return. I did this regularly on one of my large projects where none of the stakeholders had previously worked with a business analyst, and it really helped get their buy-in. It was at a project working group, and it also enabled a commitment of their time and enabled me to report back on progress.

It may also be the case that stakeholders' understanding increases over time. A good business analyst should be able to provide structure to elicit the requirements, prevent silos, gain the appropriate amount of detail, remove ambiguity about requirements and ensure consensus.

Building a communication plan

You will find it useful to put a communication plan together to structure relationships and encourage communication. This is where you will need to list each of your stakeholders, along with their roles, contact details and amount of interest in the project, and a plan of how to engage them and how often. Once you understand the frequency of contact you think you need, organize an informal chat with the stakeholders, and agree and confirm the contact and what you will cover each time. Then ensure you get the regular agreed meetings booked in the diaries. This will make life so much easier, as a regular routine is established with the contact you need.

Getting early involvement

One of the most common problems for a business analyst is not being involved early enough on in the project. Being involved early on means you can build relationships earlier and have a better understanding of the stakeholder journey. It can be harder if the stakeholders think they have given all the required information before you are involved. It's even more difficult if developers have already been engaged, because stakeholders often have a perception that a business analyst may then hold things up.

Early collaboration with architects, developers or third party suppliers will enable an earlier understanding of solution options and a better understanding of costs for the business case. It will also help ensure there is a consistent, joined-up view and mean you are better able to deal with issues when challenged if you are working closely together. It will also help promote the big picture view and how everything needs to fit together.

Building rapport

If you are likeable, stakeholders are more likely to make time for you. Make sure you introduce yourself, ask about them and take an interest in what they say. Take seriously any concerns they have and always respond promptly to them. Don't always have formal meetings; sometimes accidentally passing by their desk and having an informal conversation or inviting them for a tea or coffee can gain far more information.

You must be able to build a good relationship and a cooperative and trusting partnership. Ideally the way to do this is to find out the names of those who should be your direct contacts and establish yourself as a person they can trust to talk to for information they may need. This is especially applicable with third parties. I have seen so many projects go wrong when third parties talk directly to the business representatives and the business analyst gets left out. Being proactive, knowing the names and phone numbers of the key third party contacts and making known to them how you can help them and what your role is will make the relationship much easier.

Think about whether and how often you need to talk to each of your stakeholders and set up regular meetings in advance in calendars to help maintain the contact if necessary. Building trust is important and needs to work both ways. If you feel you don't understand why something is being done a particular way, ask questions to find out the other person's viewpoint.

Planning and estimating work

You must feel empowered and have techniques for estimating as part of collaborating well with the project manager. It will not bode well for having a good relationship with your stakeholders if you knowingly or unknowingly miss deadlines when planning and an early discussion would have enabled an agreement to be reached or additional support or other options to be considered.

The project manager may have overall responsibility for the project plan, but the business analyst is responsible for providing the business analysis activities and estimated effort to feed into the plan. If alignment isn't done between the project manager and the business analyst there may be a mismatch. This could mean unplanned delays to the project and impact the quality of the requirements. The sooner discussions can be had about the achievability of, and the time required for, the business analysis deliverables the easier it is resolve any issues.

Planning how much time you will need with the stakeholders will also help set out their expectations, gain their agreement and make it easier for them to plan their time to accommodate the project.

EXAMPLE

I was asked to deliver a signed-off business requirements document within six weeks for a large project. When I went through my estimates I realized I needed to engage with four different business areas and 12 different subject matter experts, and there were six different workstreams in scope. In addition, the stakeholders had told me they didn't know what their requirements were because it involved incorporating brand new processes they had no experience of. This meant I needed to run workshops to understand and gain consensus on the 'to be' processes first. Going through the amount of engagement I needed with the project manager enabled him to support me with getting the meetings set up with all the relevant stakeholders and enforce the message on the importance of attendance.

Providing early feedback

It is useful to be the first person to review the outputs from the design and development phases against the requirements prior to the business stakeholders seeing them. This allows business analysts to offer early feedback to the developer and third parties and provides the opportunity for any changes to be made prior to the business seeing the outcome. This will help ensure the business's expectations are met based on the requirements and improve its confidence.

Arranging walkthroughs

Always offer to conduct walkthroughs of your documentation with each of your stakeholders to answer any of their questions and to get their immediate feedback. This will demonstrate to stakeholders that their input is valued and that as a business analyst you are open to their opinions.

How do you change your communication approach to meet the needs of your stakeholders?

Everyone does not think or learn in the same way. This is why you need to recognize the importance of adapting your communication style depending upon your audience. This will help build rapport with and influence your stakeholders. There are six different types of modality for how people experience things. The ways in which they experience impacts how they think. This will vary over time, so it is important to recognize the modality being favoured by a person at a moment in time and adapt accordingly.

'Modality' is another word for 'sense' and is concerned with how we navigate through the world. There are six modalities:

- visuality;
- sound;
- feeling;
- smell;
- taste;
- logic.

We will all use these senses but will tend to prefer one over the other.

Some may prefer to see a picture, some need to hear how to do it, some need to get a feeling for it and others may need to make logical sense of it. It is more unusual for someone's primary modality to be related to smell or taste, so I do not cover these ones in any more detail.

Many professions already incorporate these different styles of thinking and learning as good standard practice. Training companies ensure their course uses pictures for those who are more visual, the spoken word for those who respond better to sound, materials printed out for those who go by their feelings, and exercises for those who are primarily driven through logically working things out. In the car sales industry a car salesperson will show potential car buyers around the car to give them a visual picture, get them to sit in the car to get a feel for it, start the engine to hear it and explain details to enable them to make more sense of it.

One of my favourite stories for demonstrating how it can make a difference is about the experience of one of my friends in a hi-fi store. She had seen what she described to the salesperson as a great-looking hi-fi in the window. The salesperson explained that it didn't have good-quality sound or a high sampling frequency. He then took my friend to look at a different hi-fi and explained how she needed a sampling frequency of 96kHz or 192kHZ at 24 bit. My friend explained she didn't like the look of it. The assistant then went on about the cables and transistors. My friend ended up leaving the store feeling disappointed that she couldn't buy a hi-fi she liked. I imagine the sales assistant was disappointed that he didn't make a sale. If the salesperson had known anything about different modalities he should have realized from my friend's opening line, 'I've seen a great-looking hi-fi in the window', that her primary modality was visual. Not surprisingly his preference was audio. But I can't help but think that if he had realized how appearance mattered more to her then he would have got that sale.

So how does this relate to business analysis? Once you can recognize the primary modalities being used by your stakeholders you can adapt your communication approach. If stakeholders' primary modality is sight they will respond better to scene setting and diagrams. If they are driven by sounds and listening they will prefer to be talked through something. If they like to get in touch with how they feel they will want to get a feel for the subject being talked about and might need to have a view of the subject matter in advance. If they have a preference for logically making sense of their situation they will also want an early view so they can logically work out what they think.

One of the reasons I always send a clear agenda out with stated objectives before a meeting is that it works better for those who prefer to get a feeling or make logical sense of a subject. The more time I can give them to think about it or work out how they feel the more contribution I will get in the meeting. In my work with IT and with actuaries I have observed that by the nature of their profession they are very logical thinkers and things must make sense.

One of the reasons why I use diagrams in meetings is to keep up with the speed of those with a primary visual modality. They will think quickly because they are thinking in pictures. It helps also to slow them down, because it gives them a chance to explain how the picture in their head might be different to what I have drawn up on the board. I also tend to use diagrams in much of my documentation, because they will find this easier than lots of words and it is more likely to hold their attention.

One of the reasons why I talk people through and ensure everyone gets their say is to benefit those who favour the sound modality. It is easier for them to talk through and listen to ideas, as they are thinking in words. I always offer a walkthrough of my documentation so they can hear it.

The notion that people will always favour one modality is unlikely to be true, and people's preference will vary over time and depending upon what they are doing. However, the idea of modality is useful in understanding that you do need to vary your approach and have some awareness of what you need to do differently depending upon the situation and what modalities your stakeholders are favouring at a moment in time.

Modality is most noticeable when people are learning something new. When I was coaching some trainee business analysts I had one who didn't get it if I explained it to her but if I got her to do an exercise then she could work it out. For another I had to draw pictures and explain concepts to give the big picture first. There was another for whom talking it through worked best. If I hadn't understood why I needed to treat them differently I wouldn't have got as much out of them.

We are so dependent on getting information to understand requirements from our stakeholders or getting their buy-in that the more effective we are at doing this the more success we will have.

What do you do when stakeholders go straight to the solution without explaining the context or vision?

There may be occasions where your stakeholders get focused on what solutions they would like, and it may be beneficial to understand the wider context first. This is a brief summary of some questions you can ask to help understand this.

These are the common situations where you will be able to use this technique:

- to identify opportunities and benefits where they are unclear or not yet defined;
- to uncover justifications behind requirements;
- when writing a business case or vision document;

- if stakeholders go straight to the solution and you need a technique to uncover the business requirement behind it;

- if stakeholders go into detail and you need to understand the context and bigger picture first.

It is a simple technique and just consists of remembering four questions:

- What is the purpose?
- What is your intention?
- What is this an example of?
- What does having this give you that is more important?

Asking any of these four questions will help when a stakeholder is providing you with information and you need to understand more about the context. The four questions all have the same effect. It just so happens that if you remember more than one it prevents asking the same question if you need to keep understanding the meaning behind the stakeholder's answer.

Why is getting requirements/information from stakeholders so difficult and how do you overcome it?

Our stakeholders will always have a more complete internal representation of what they wish to communicate than what they can put into words. Therefore, they will shorten the description. This leads to generalizing information, deleting most of the material or distorting it.

There are other good reasons why people do this. They must generalize to a certain extent. Generalizing helps us to learn quickly so we do not have to relearn old concepts. This allows us to compare and generalize old similar material with new data. People must also delete some of the information they give. Every second millions of pieces of information feed into the brain, so it makes sense that we screen out much of this information. In addition, people distort to simplify the description of their experience.

The impact this has on the business analyst is that the person giving the requirements may have missed out important information, distorted the information and given generalizations without being specific. The same might apply to you without you realizing it when you write a business requirements document. I regularly review my documentation to look out for signs that I have done this. I will provide you with some guidance on how to recognize it and what questions to ask to resolve it.

If we don't try to remove ambiguity, then the requirements gathered will be subject to many different interpretations, especially as they get handed over to different teams such as development and testing.

The result could then be project failure, where what is delivered does not match the stakeholders' needs or the benefits expected. There could be massive delays to the project, where sign-offs are delayed or lots of questions still need to be answered from the developers, testers, third parties or others.

Overcoming generalizations, information not provided or distorted information is why gathering requirements is so difficult.

Read the following requirements and decide for yourself before reading any further whether and how these requirements can be improved or what questions could be asked to ensure information is not missing:

- All remittance advice notes must be emailed.
- No one should ever have command line access to the live system.
- Everyone should be able to access the system.
- The requirement should have a priority of 'essential'.
- The human resources (HR) file should be processed daily.
- Data needs to be sent quarterly.
- The system must be the fastest on the market.
- The system must be user friendly.

Generalizations

There are three types of generalizations to look out for. I'll explain each one in turn and which parts of the requirements above use language that signifies where each type of generalization is being used.

1 The first type of generalization assumes that one situation applies to every scenario. Words that indicate this are 'all', 'every', 'never', 'no one' and similar.

   – *All* remittance advice notes must be emailed.

   – *No one* should ever have command line access to the live system.

   – *Everyone* should be able to access the system.

   To overcome this, find a counter-example. For example, are there any circumstances where remittance advice notes will not be emailed?

2 The second type of generalization is where a rule is implied without an explanation or clarification of why it is a rule. There may not be a rule, and not exploring this could unfairly limit what is possible. The cause of this needs to be understood. Words that indicate this type of generalization are 'should', 'shouldn't', 'must', 'must not', 'have to', 'need to' and 'it is necessary', as well as words of possibility/impossibility such as 'can'/'can't', 'will'/'won't', 'may'/'may not' and 'possible'/'impossible'.

- All remittance advice notes *must* be emailed.
- No one *should* ever have command line access to the live system.
- Everyone *should* be able to access the system.
- The requirement *should* have a priority of 'essential'.
- The HR file *should* be processed daily.
- The system *must* be the fastest on the market.
- The system *must* be user friendly.

To overcome this, you must clarify the cause of the rule. For example, why must remittance notes be emailed?

3 The third type of generalization is where assumptions have been made that one thing will cause another to happen. This is more likely to come up in spoken language and be hidden when the requirement is written down. When the requirements are written down, go through each one and ask yourself if there are any assumptions made.

- The HR file should be processed daily.

It is important to recover the source, ask about the assumed ideas and gather evidence. For example, what if there isn't an HR file?

Deletion

There are four types of deletions to look out for. I'll explain each one in turn and which parts of the requirements stated earlier use language that signifies where each type of deletion has occurred.

1 The first type is simple deletion, where a statement is made but information is missing from it.

- All *remittance advice notes* must be *emailed*.
- No one should ever have command line access to the live *system*.
- Everyone should be able to *access* the *system*.

- The requirement should have a priority of '*essential*'.
- The *HR file* should be *processed* daily.
- The *system* must be the *fastest* on the *market*.
- The *system* must be *user friendly*.

There are several items of information missing from the requirements above. It is necessary to uncover the deleted information. For example, what systems are being referred to, what is the HR file, where is it, what format is it in and what is meant by 'user friendly'?

2   The second type of deletion is when a reference point is missing. Words used might be 'good', 'better', 'best', 'worst', 'more', 'less', 'most' and 'least'. When this happens, you must identify and recover the unstated comparison.

3   The third type of deletion is when there is an unstated reference, such as when a person or thing is specified. For example, if the word 'they' is used then you would need to ask who is referred to by 'they'. This identifies the unstated reference.

4   The fourth type of deletion is when a verb is used but the person doing the acting or desired action is left out. This means you would need to identify that person.

Distortion

There are five types of distortions. Distortions can taint beliefs and attitudes. They are also a good source of resistance in communication. I'll cover them, as you may find them useful. However, I would recommend exercising caution and instinct as to whether it is appropriate to ask the type of questions needed to uncover the distortions straight away, as some of these could be quite emotive.

1   The first type of distortion is when process words are frozen in time, for example 'I'm going to'. When this happens there are additional questions needed to convert the words to include what the actual action needs to be.

2   The second type of distortion is when a link is made from a cause to an action without an explanation of why the cause and action are linked. When this happens further questions are needed as to why the statements made are related.

3 The third type of distortion is claiming to know someone's internal state. Words to look out for are terms like 'they', for example where something is specified without reference to how the conclusion was formed. This could indicate that assumptions had been made without the validity of the claim being clear. Only by understanding how people came to their view will it be possible to know whether their statement has been distorted by their beliefs. For example, when relationships break down at work this can sometimes be attributed to a lack of trust where the impacted stakeholders may believe they know what the other person is thinking, which may or may not be true.

4 The fourth type of distortion is when two unrelated statements are represented as equivalent. The statement 'I won't give you our requirements; IT never deliver what we want' is an example of complex equivalence. This is something I mentioned in Chapter 1 in relation to an incident that happened early on in my career. I could have challenged the person by asking whether IT could deliver the requirements without the person giving me the requirements. As it happened, I chose the more subtle approach of relocating my desk near the person so I could build up trust.

5 The fifth type of distortion is when a value judgement is made, such as it being wrong to do something. When this happens there is a need to identify the source and criteria.

How do you run a workshop/meeting effectively?

Running meetings is not easy and takes considerable skill and experience to master. I regularly think that getting all the stakeholders I need into a room is a bit like herding cats. They are all independent thinkers and have different meeting schedules and different needs. They may turn up, not turn up, be late, wander off at different times and have other distractions. You may get some more dominating characters than others and different levels of participation. You could also end up with the more dominating characters wanting to pursue their own agendas or wanting to change the topics you had in mind. You might also encounter conflict if the attendees do not agree with each other or even with yourself. If any of these happen there is a real danger of running out of time or not getting what you wanted from the meeting.

Over the years I have put together a list of best practice tips to avoid or reduce the problems covered above.

Agenda

Make sure you are clear what you want to achieve from the meeting and what you will need to cover as a result. A simple way to do this is to create an agenda for the meeting. The agenda will normally be one page. Your company may already have an agenda template you can use with its own corporate branding. If not, it is important to include the following information:

- The heading of the document must be clearly labelled 'Agenda' at the top, along with the date of the meeting and location.
- This will be followed by a list of all who have been invited and are known to be expected. Provide a separate list of those who have sent their apologies and will not be able to attend.
- Then summarize the objective of the meeting in no more than a couple of sentences.
- A table follows listing the order of items you want to discuss along with who is involved with each and how long should be spent on it.
- As a standard you may want the first few agenda items to be introductions and overview.
- You may also want to end the agenda with next steps and any other business.

An agenda makes sure that all the attendees know in advance what you want to achieve from the meeting. It enables them to prepare for it and to let you know if they think anyone is missing from the attendee list or whether there is anything they believe should be added as an item for discussion. It will also enable them to speak out if they feel they cannot contribute so you can have a chat with them in advance to agree whether they should attend or not.

Another powerful reason for sending out an agenda in advance is that you can use it to prevent stakeholders taking the meeting off topic. If this happens it is then easier to say 'Let's take this offline, as it isn't on the agenda.' It can then be covered at the end under 'any other business' or added as a car park item (see 'Car park' below in this section).

Including time slots in the agenda is a good way of keeping the meeting on track to prevent running out of time. This will help retain focus on a topic and enable the participants to help you keep to the allotted time. You could give the responsibility to one of the participants to act as time-keeper and to let you know when each topic needs to start being wrapped up.

Pre-meeting informal catch-ups

When applicable, have smaller informal catch-up meetings prior to running a larger meeting. This is most useful at the beginning of a project or if you and the stakeholder concerned do not know each other very well. This enables stakeholders to ask questions about the agenda and objectives to make sure they are comfortable with what needs to be covered. It will help build rapport and trust, because individuals will feel as though they are more involved and have a say. It gives them the opportunity to provide you with more ideas that may help develop your agenda and gain their buy-in. Some people are also more comfortable in an informal setting and may open up more if their managers are not in the room.

Meeting room set-up

If possible, arrange access to the room prior to the meeting. This will enable you to set up the meeting room. You may want to check you can access the equipment you need, such as a computer, projector screen, flip charts and pens. You may also want some time to stick paper on the wall in advance if you want to have specific headings. Good practice is to have the following available as headings on flip chart paper on the wall: 'car park', 'actions', 'dependencies', 'risks', 'assumptions' and 'issues'. The term 'car park' is covered later in this section. These are all things that might come up during a meeting that are not necessarily planned. This way they can be captured as and when they happen and can easily be added to if required. Think about whether you need to take some of the following types of equipment with you: adhesive tack, sticky tape, scissors, pens for the whiteboard, pens for flip charts and sticky notes. Some companies and teams put together a work-shop kit to cover this for you. If a meeting is two hours or more find out whether you can arrange refreshments, including tea, coffee, water, biscuits, sweets and chocolate. Doing this as standard will also encourage attendance for future meetings.

Checking attendance

Check with the attendees that they can make the date and time being proposed for the meeting. It may be worth confirming the day as well. Stakeholders are more likely to ensure they attend if they have promised to do so verbally beforehand. It also gives them a chance to let you know if they cannot make it at that time, so a more convenient time can be arranged. If they cannot attend it also gives them an opportunity to suggest a deputy.

Introductions

Setting the scene at the beginning of the meeting and creating a relaxed environment can make a huge difference to how much people contribute. It is important that the attendees feel comfortable in contributing, especially if there are many attendees. People need to know who is in the room and what their roles are. If you know some attendees are likely to be quiet, ask everyone as part of their introduction to state why they are there, what they want to get out of the meeting and what they are going to contribute. The attendees should know from the agenda you sent out and your pre-meeting catch-ups what the purpose of the meeting is. If they do not know why they are there they will be grateful to get some time back in their diary and you can carry on without them. It is better for this to be realized at the beginning of the meeting and not when people have sat through a meeting unnecessarily.

Using flip charts, sticky notes and visual aids

Writing outputs down on flip charts throughout the meeting will help ensure the attendees agree with what you have written and that you all have the same interpretation. It will also give attendees the opportunity to reflect and add more detail. It is normally worth reading through all the outputs on the flip charts prior to the meeting finishing to give time for reflection and to check understanding. If there are opportunities to draw diagrams, then this will also be advantageous. Diagrams tend to make things very black and white, so any ambiguity can be cleared up straight away.

EXAMPLE

A powerful technique for ensuring participation can be to hand out sticky notes and pens. Ask everyone to write down their thoughts on a subject area you wish to know about. After people have written out their sticky notes they should be asked to stick them up on the wall so they can view each other's ideas. This is a great method for getting quieter members to contribute and share their knowledge and ideas. It also prevents the favouring of the highest-paid person's opinion (HiPPO). It is often worth getting different perspectives, as the person doing the work may have a different view to the person higher up the hierarchy.

Another reason for writing out and visually showing the output to everyone during the meeting is to slow down the pace. Doing this will help you to capture everything, as stakeholders then realize if they are talking too fast or need to provide you with further information. It's no use getting to the end of the meeting and realizing afterwards that you didn't understand what your stakeholders were talking about.

Car park

Have a piece of flip chart paper with 'Car park' written on it and use it to record discussions that come up that aren't part of the objectives of the workshop. This really helps give you control of the meeting and prevents it from going off topic. When someone brings up a subject you don't want to cover then you can say to them: 'This isn't part of the agenda for this meeting. We will capture it in the car park so it isn't forgotten about. We will then deal with it separately to this meeting.' What you will find is that once your stakeholders are used to this concept the workshop will become self-governing, as stakeholders will then know to ask to have items added to the car park without going too off topic. If you don't control the meeting in this way you could end up running out of time and realizing you haven't covered what you wanted to.

Using silence

Use silence, especially after asking a question. It can be tempting to want to fill in awkward silences. This is the very reason why you sometimes must resist the temptation to speak. This will enable your stakeholders to fill in the silence instead and enable you to get more information from them. It might be best to make anyone accompanying you aware of this, especially if they are not people you need to get information from, as they might feel the need to speak instead. This is an especially great technique for getting people to put their name down against actions.

Agreeing actions and next steps

Make sure you allow at least 10 minutes towards the end of a meeting to review the actions needed and to discuss the next steps. Ensure all actions are written up, ideally in everyone's view, with an assigned name and a target completion date. Also gain agreement as to whether another meeting is required, who to involve and for how long. This is helpful to ensure buy-in for any further help required from people.

Minuting meetings

After the meeting write up minutes to include the key decisions and actions. Then distribute the minutes to all the stakeholders involved, asking them to review and provide updates or amendments. It also gives you the opportunity to include other stakeholders who couldn't make the meeting or who have a vested interest in it. It will also help ensure that the project risks, assumptions, issues and dependencies (RAID) log is updated. Minutes are very important to make sure that key decisions are documented so they can be evidenced if necessary. It enables stakeholders to help you if they realize something has been missed or misunderstood. It makes sure everyone has the same understanding. Actions from the minutes can then be tracked, with emails sent out to chase and close the actions agreed.

03

Business context and vision

Introduction

Business context is about the current situation and environment. The vision is about what the business wants to achieve and how its success can be measured. Outlining the business context and vision at the beginning of the business analysis process is essential, as combined these concepts set out the direction of change.

If the business context and vision are determined incorrectly, the consequences can make it difficult to elicit and document the requirements for the business analyst, agree the solution for the architects and estimate and keep to a plan for the project manager. It also makes it more difficult for the business stakeholders to understand what they are getting out of the process and to develop a common consensus. Therefore, it is essential that the following are established before a project is agreed:

- problems and opportunities;
- scope;
- stakeholders required;
- constraints and dependencies that need to be adhered to;
- areas of change;
- end to end business processes impacted;
- solution options; and
- recommended approach.

Guidance provided in this chapter will help utilize your understanding of the business context and vision of any company to avoid common pitfalls. For example, sizing business change incorrectly and failing to distinguish between small and large change or small, medium, large and very large projects stem from a lack of context and vision and can cause issues.

Questions covered in this chapter about setting business context and vision

This chapter answers the following questions:

- How do you know you are solving the right problem?
- How do you gain consensus for the direction of the project and its scope with all stakeholders?
- How do you go about identifying all your stakeholders?
- How do you identify constraints that might influence the solution?
- How do you identify the needs that might influence the solution?
- How do you ensure the overall solution agreed will meet the business needs?
- How do you justify the benefits and estimated costs?

How do you know you are solving the right problem?

The importance of determining the nature and scope of a problem should not be understated. Understanding problems at the beginning of a project is essential in making sure the requirements and solutions will resolve the issues and realize the opportunities. Failure to do so can result in problems not being solved in their entirety or being moved somewhere else or other issues developing. It is the responsibility of the business analyst to ensure traceability throughout a project, and understanding the problem is one of the first stages that needs to be understood.

When the problem is not correctly addressed there will be indicators, such as unclear proposed solutions with frequent going backward and forward and lots of detail without any context. In these cases, often there will be a need to look beyond the perceived problem and to investigate the root causes of the actual problem. Changes must have a purpose and have a basis for being proposed. Once the problem is understood it is far easier to offer solutions based on evidence.

It is very difficult to come up with solutions or be innovative if the essence of the problem is not ascertained first. This chapter introduces several techniques to help understand the problem. If the solution is chosen too early, then opportunities can be missed and traceability back to whether the problem has been resolved will be difficult.

There are several techniques for understanding the problems, which this section will cover, to help our stakeholders make informed decisions. Stakeholders will tend to have different perspectives, because they have a variety of experiences and pain points, so individually they may not have a full understanding of the problems. However, getting all stakeholders together allows different viewpoints to be brought together and a full picture to be obtained.

Problem identification method 1 – problem statements

Problem statements highlight the reasons for needing a change and set out what the problems are that need resolving. They are normally a few paragraphs in stakeholders' own words describing what the problems are, what impact they have, the size of the problems and some measurements for understanding what is important to them for the change to be a success. Problem statements explore the pain points that stakeholders face and what causes them difficulties. These difficulties are normally the most visible to stakeholders so make a good starting point towards understanding the context and vision.

Having clear problem statements provides a success criterion to measure the project against. It will also help in understanding the cost and consequences of not doing the project, as all the problems would remain unresolved, and the impact and effect of the project would be unrealized. It might be the case that the business can live with the problems and may decide not to pursue the changes, because there could be other projects that will have a bigger impact and hence a higher priority. It also could be because when the costs are estimated it is decided that they do not provide as much benefit as to make the problems worth resolving. Understanding the problem statement makes it easier to judge how big the problems are and enables better understanding of priorities against other competing projects. Every company has a limited budget and resources and lots of possible projects to implement change. The problem statement helps people to understand the business context to allow comparisons and to get an idea of urgency.

Regularly revisiting problem statements throughout projects ensures that the requirements and solutions being approved relate back and that there are no gaps. It is possible that further problems have been identified or requirements and solutions proposed. It will also help to prioritize the requirements, because each requirement should relate back to a problem. If it doesn't then the requirement can be challenged as to whether it really is required. It is more difficult to challenge how much a requirement is needed if the problem it is meant to resolve is not clear.

EXAMPLE

I apply this method when my stakeholders already feel as though they have a clear understanding of the problems or if they have already been thinking or writing about requirements or solutions.

I place flip chart paper on the walls and ask them the following questions:

- What is the problem and why?
- What is the impact?
- Who does it affect and when?
- What would success look like?

Throughout the meeting I suggest you add the answers to these continually as more thought is put into it. During this exercise it will be natural for stakeholders to think about solutions, but it is your responsibility as facilitator to bring them back to the problem statement. Using a flip chart to capture car park items, as outlined in Chapter 2, may help with this to move the conversation on.

When discussing the problems, you may find it useful to regularly ask why and what it means to stakeholders. This will help identify root causes rather than just symptoms. Understanding when problems occur will also help identify the trigger points and the severity for each area of the business. It is important to cover this question at different levels of stakeholder in the organization, as they will have different viewpoints.

There are many different types of impact caused by a problem that can be listed on a problem statement. These could be financial or regulatory or relate to processes, capability, services, systems or staff numbers, for example. The impact could also vary based on size and severity. In understanding the impact, it is worth exploring what would happen if nothing was done about it. The number of times the problem occurs and the frequency of the problems will also help towards understanding the impact. If the volumes and frequency are low, then the impact may be lower compared to high volumes and high frequency. Understanding this will influence the solutions available and determine their suitability, for example manual or automated solutions.

Who a problem affects also needs to be explored in the problem statement. This will demonstrate the complexity and the scope of problems. The problems affecting the direct stakeholders in the room may be clearer than those affecting external stakeholders such as customers in the marketplace. If this is the case, then it may be useful to explore some of the other methods. Knowing when a problem arises is useful for understanding the trigger points and the business processes impacted.

Outlining a success criterion in a problem statement is useful for understanding what is required of a successful solution and really helps stakeholders to think about what is most important to them. Getting this right will really help to prioritize the requirements later. It will help to discount solutions and will provide traceability to ensure the solution when being delivered still meets these criteria.

Problem identification method 2 – process modelling analysis

Process modelling will be covered in more detail in Chapter 4. However, this is an effective method of problem identification that will be introduced here. Process modelling can be used to identify problems and opportunities by documenting and analysing the 'as is' business processes.

I have used a standard industry modelling notation called Business Process Model and Notation (BPMN), which will also be explained in greater detail in Chapter 4 along with notations to explain each symbol. It is intuitive, but you should always provide an explanation of the symbols each time you use it. Process modelling offers several benefits over other approaches. If the processes go over several business areas, the stakeholders may only know their own business area. This will disguise any problems with the overall end to end process. Making each business area's process visible will enable conversations between the different areas and highlight which processes may cause problems further down the line. It will also show where there are delays between business areas and unnecessary handoffs.

If people are used to doing tasks the same way for a long period of time they might not perceive all the problems. Issues and their workarounds become ingrained and commonplace. Inviting stakeholders to take a step back and view their processes will help them to see the bigger picture.

Once the 'as is' process is documented it can then be reviewed to discuss the pain points in each process. This will generate further questions to enable understanding of the impact of some of the findings. Understanding the problems in the processes will enable an understanding of how to improve the processes.

Modelling processes provides the ability to dig deeper into which of the processes cause problems, the impact of them and who this affects. It then enables a conversation as to which processes should fall within the scope for change.

Once you have mapped out the end to end process you can add information to each process to understand more about potential problems and impacts. This can include:

- the length of time each process takes and the effort behind it;
- the time taken between each process;
- the volumes behind each process;
- the success criteria of each process;
- alternative flows for each process, especially if not successful;
- a statement of what processes have inputs or outputs as documentation, including naming them;
- a statement of whether each process is manual, involves interaction with a computer system or is automated.

These suggestions will help towards understanding the success criteria and the scope of the change required. For example, if volumes are low then the impact could be low and not worth resolving or less of a priority.

CASE STUDY

Let's take an example of a marketing team in a fictional company called Dream Phones who want to send out targeted marketing messages for selling their mobile phones.

The process in Figure 3.1 shows the marketing team request details each month from the sales team. The sales team receive the request, retrieve the customer details and send them back to the marketing team. On receiving the customer details the marketing team then request a list of available stock from the procurement team.

FIGURE 3.1 Business process model (using BPMN)

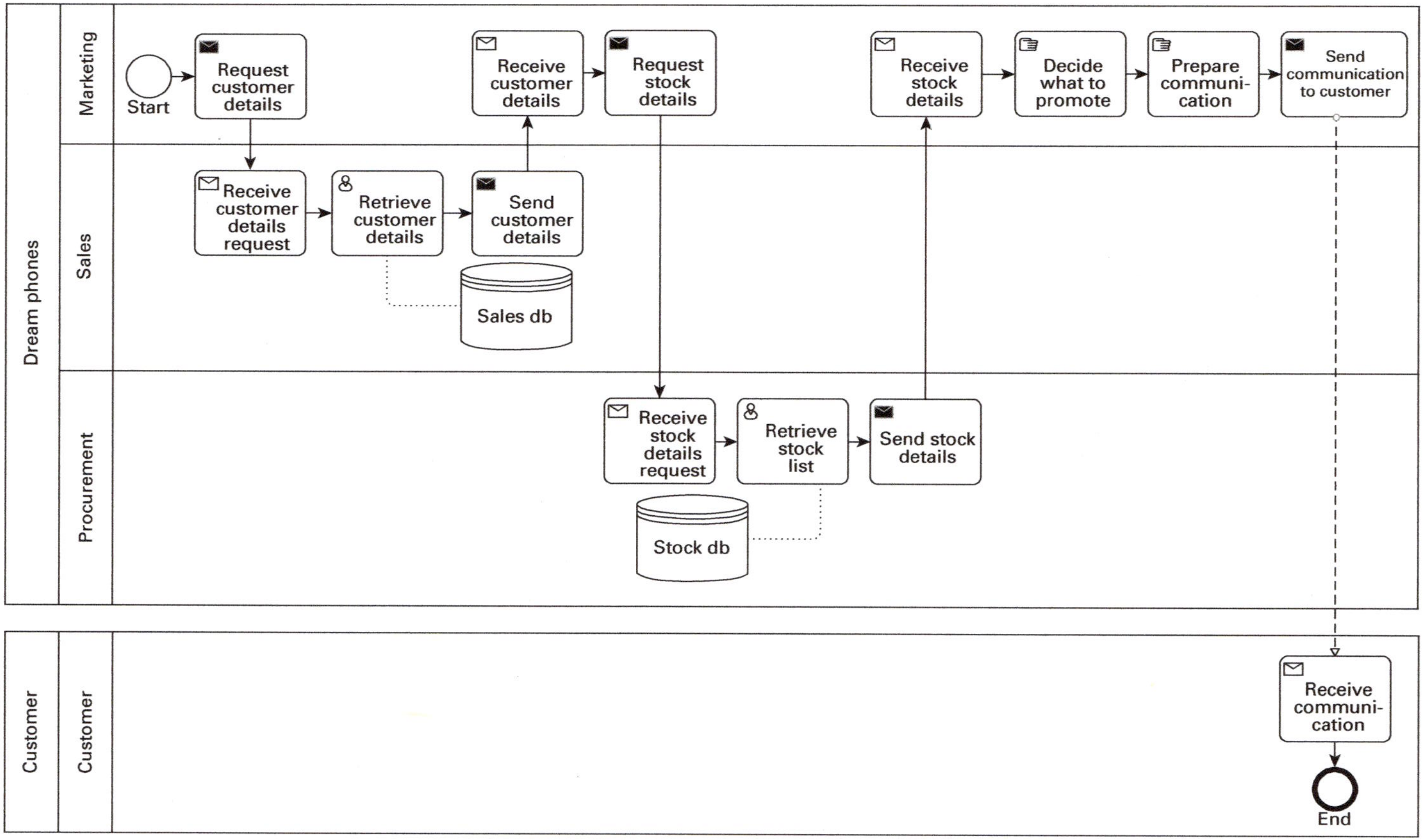

The procurement team, on receiving the request, retrieve the stock list and send the details back to the sales team. Once the marketing team have a list of the stock available, they can then decide what to promote, prepare a communication and send the communication out to the customer. The customer at the end of the process then receives the communication of the products being marketed to him or her. You might want to compare the description of the processes in this paragraph with Figure 3.1. It is much easier to see any ambiguity in the figure and to fill any gaps compared to reading the narrative. The figure is also faster to draw, making it easier to populate in a workshop.

The following observations can be drawn from this case study:

- The marketing team must wait for information from the sales and procurement teams before they can make decisions on what products to promote each month and identify the customers to communicate with.

Therefore, it would be useful to find out about the time it takes to receive the required information from the other teams to enable understanding of the impact this has and whether it causes any problems. In addition, how much time and effort do other teams spend collating the information? Are these existing reports that have little impact, or is there an amount of regular effort required? Why does each team have to wait to be asked for this information if it is required every month? As soon as the stakeholders understand how each other's involvement works in a process it may lead to improvements that can be handled in their business as usual processes rather than a project and be a quick win.

- The marketing team cannot analyse what to promote until towards the end of the process.

Marketing is dependent on what stock is available rather than focused on the interests of the customer.

- The marketing team relies on customer details that might be out of date.

There is the possibility that customer details provided at the point of sale could quickly become out of date. There appears to be no process for updating these details. All these examples could cause problems.

The success criteria can then be defined so as to understand what it is important for the business to obtain from the project. Examples from this case study could be:

- to have a list of customers stored centrally that can be accessed by both sales and marketing;
- to use other mediums for gathering customer details rather than just at the point of sale;

- to be able to report on the success of customers who have taken up the offer based on the marketing carried out;

- to enable procurement to purchase stock based on demand generated from marketing initiatives, for example.

Care must be exercised not to generate too many constraints for success, so discussions must be focused on what is most important.

Problem identification method 3 – analysing existing systems or data

Analysing the systems and data is another method for ensuring the problems are identified and resolved throughout the project. The reason for this analysis is to check the data and systems behave in the way expected. This will require the ability to analyse data and to understand the structure and relationships between the data. There are several reporting tools that can be used if needed to view the data without having to know programming languages to access data.

Questions to ask yourself during this analysis are:

- Does the system work as the business expects?
- How reliable and accurate are the data?
- Are the data structured in a way that allows data to be obtained in the way expected?
- Can the data be obtained from one source and, if not, what are the different sources?
- Is there any manual intervention, how much and from whom?
- How often is the system updated?
- What transformations or calculations are performed on the data and when?
- How well are the data understood?
- Is there a data owner responsible for updating and maintaining changes to the system?
- Are the fields used for the purpose for which they were originally intended?

Answers to these questions may reveal a multitude of problems. However, certain problems may not be significant enough to be resolved, especially those that do not have major impacts. Budgets are a factor.

To understand if the system is working as expected, you need to understand how the business uses the system and the business rules. It will then involve checking whether this matches what the system does by walking through with technical stakeholders, who have ideally been involved in the systems design or development. If the business has had to introduce lots of manual workarounds after a system has been delivered, then this could show that the system isn't working as originally expected or that the problems originally envisaged aren't resolved.

Business stakeholders will be able to tell you about the reliability and accuracy of the data. If the data are not reliable and accurate then there may be high levels of manual intervention to correct this.

If there isn't a data owner responsible for updating and maintaining changes to the system, it will be more difficult to keep the system up to date with any new data requirements. There is then more of a chance that, when new data are required, redundant fields are used to fill the gap instead of new ones. This might not be a problem in the short term. However, the field description will not match what the business is using it for. As time goes by it may become a problem, as it will make system changes more complicated in terms of understanding the data for those who are not regular users.

Problem identification method 4 – design thinking

Design thinking puts the customer experience at the heart of the analysis when looking at how to resolve or understand problems. Design thinking is important, because it does not focus on streamlining processes or making use of new technology. It instead looks at how the customer experience can be improved by using existing technology but in a different way. Uber, Amazon, Facebook, Twitter, Google, Airbnb and Netflix are all companies that have been created or have grown substantially since 2010. These are companies that have put the customer experience at the centre of their strategy and developed new ways of providing experiences or products.

Below are some example design thinking techniques all of which benefit from conducting research, making observations and sourcing a range of people with different backgrounds and experiences to contribute.

PERSONAS

The techniques of creating 'personas' involves observing customers' actual experiences and trying to gain an insight into the lives of the customers. Based on observation and research, user personas can be created to represent the different groups of individuals who interact with your product or service. A persona is an imaginary customer but one who matches the demographics and interests of who you would consider to be a typical customer. You may choose to come up with three to five different personas to ensure you cover the range of people with whom the product or service provided might engage.

Give each persona a real name, as you want the exercise to feel as real as possible so as to be able to engage with and feel empathetic to this person. You need to be able to add enough detail to the personas so you can see things from their perspective. This means providing demographic details and their goals and frustrations with your product so you can see their experiences from their own viewpoint.

CASE STUDY

Let's go back to the previous fictional company, Dream Phones, which sells mobile phones. Figure 3.2 provides an example of a persona to describe a typical customer. Such descriptions provide personas' demographic details, their goals about how they want to use mobile phones, their behaviour, their frustrations and a short biography. This is to help give Dream Phones an insight into how their customers are feeling and how they want to interact when buying or using a mobile phone. This could influence the services and types of phone the company should be offering.

FIGURE 3.2 Persona

NAME – TONY SUMMERS

Photo

AGE: 43

GENDER: Male

OCCUPATION: Web Designer

GOALS:
- To have the latest technology
- To have really good quality photos that can be shared online
- Has to have good performance
- Usability

BEHAVIOUR:
- Replaces phone every year
- Uses the camera features
- Uses satellite navigation
- Plays lots of group games
- Likes a good deal

FRUSTRATIONS:
- The speed of phone
- Availability of the phones you might be interested in
- Colour choice
- Lack of offers
- Pre-installed apps that are not required

BIO:
Tony loves playing games on his phone in his spare time. Tony is a keen photographer and likes to take photos of wildlife. He likes to go on weekends away to the seaside. He always wants to have the latest technology.

CUSTOMER JOURNEYS

Once personas have been identified you can chart the stages imagined customers go through when buying your company's service or product from the points of view of what they do, how they think and how they feel. The emotions or pain points the personas go through on their journey are identified. This technique is useful for understanding the difficulties your customers may encounter and helping highlight areas where improvements can be made. In practice you could use sticky notes on the wall charting the journey of each persona and either use colours to represent good and bad experiences or use smiley and sad emojis. This helps with understanding the problems from a customer point of view and the benefits that can be obtained.

It also enables you to see the whole process a customer goes through end to end. This is a powerful technique for innovation, because it may lead to looking at a whole range of solutions that have been overlooked at different parts of the customer journey when thinking about the stages in isolation.

CASE STUDY

Going back to the Dream Phones case study the previous persona developed can be extended into a customer journey.

The customer journey shows the highest period of anxiety is around the customer planning and actioning the purchase of the phone. Dream Phones staff can look at these outcomes and work out which areas of change they could make to help the customer.

FIGURE 3.3 The customer journey

Steps	Preparing	Planning	Action	New phone
Doing	Look at current top phones	Play with possible phones	Make purchase	Set it up – transferring old apps to new phone – changing look and feel of icons and appearance – setting up screen lock – trying new ring tones
	Research current trends	Look at contract options	Sell old phone to make some money back	Configure it as wanted
	Read reviews		Buy new accessories for it – chargers – phone holders – cases – screen protectors	Try out new features – new apps – camera – new settings – unique features to device
	Check YouTube for reviews			
Thinking	When can I get a new phone?	Will the new phone be worth the money?	Is it worth as much as claimed?	Hope not disappointed
		Will it be as good as the current phone?		
		Is it worth being tied in for two years?		
Feeling	Excited 	Hope that there are newer phones with the wow factor 	Hope won't be disappointed 	Happiness and pride 
	:D	:|	:|	:D

Problem identification method 5 – systems thinking

Systems thinking is a holistic approach that examines a problem by looking at all the related component parts that could impact it. It examines the problem by analysing technology, people, organizations and processes.

Technology could involve looking at what is available, interactions required, data required and what problems relate to it.

When considering how people may interact with the work area under consideration, techniques could involve putting together a stakeholder map and investigating the 'as is' and 'to be' culture.

The organization considerations could include analysing the impact of the target operating model, for example on competitors, financial performance and the brand.

Process modelling as described throughout this book can be used to understand the whole end to end process and where problems may occur. This is very useful in understanding which areas should be in scope.

Once the different parts of technology, people, organization and processes are studied they need to be put back together again to enable an understanding of the whole problem.

Design thinking and systems thinking are very different. Design thinking focuses just on the customer, and system thinking is a more holistic approach and looks at a wider range of perspectives. They both however involve testing hypotheses and getting feedback to check resolution of the problems that have been identified.

How do you gain consensus for the direction of the project and its scope with all stakeholders?

Opportunities

In addition to understanding about the problems it is necessary to understand about the opportunities expected to make the changes worthwhile. This involves understanding about the key stakeholder's vision for the way forward and will reveal more about the business's appetite for change.

Some of the potential problems identified in the process modelling example for the fictional company Dream Phones might not be seen as problems. Does the business see an opportunity to market products to customers that they are more likely to be interested in? How important is it for the marketing to reach the customer? Is there an opportunity for the procurement team to purchase stock based on the interests of the customer?

Opportunities can also be analysed by looking at goals, objectives and the success criteria.

If a success measure was to increase sales, then the answers to the previous questions are more likely to be yes.

A 'to be' process diagram will also be useful in uncovering opportunities by asking the business where it sees improvements being made.

Regularly tracing back requirements to the opportunities and problems will ensure all of the requirements being gathered relate back. If a requirement does not, then either the requirement is not actually necessary or a problem or opportunity has been missed.

Determining the vision

The scope of a project must be understood between all stakeholders to ensure that progress is kept on track and focuses on the intended areas. A vision is required to understand what needs to be achieved. This will normally come from the sponsor for the project or an executive who understands the direction of the business and what changes are required to support it. The vision should be outcome and benefit focused and reflect the values of the company.

Establishing goals and objectives

Once the vision is understood, the goals and objectives to support and deliver the project can be drawn out. This is where decisions need to be made on how wide a scope is required for the changes being proposed. Caution must be exercised to make sure that the goals and objectives are not so large that delivering the project is put at risk. The bigger the project is, the greater the complexity that's involved and the more resources that are required. Therefore, it is more common that a restricted number of goals and objectives will be agreed. Doing this will bring benefits to the vision in a measured way to form a project or a programme of work.

Change is needed in an iterative way as a result of restrictions on budget and resources. Any changes also rely on buy-in from people and behavioural changes, which can take time. There is also a danger that if the scope is too large it will make the project so complicated and take so long to deliver it that it will be abandoned without any benefits realized. If the scope is carefully managed and agreed, benefits can be achieved sooner and lessons can then be learnt for continual improvement, allowing further phases to be developed later.

Traceability

Anyone involved in change needs to understand the vision. The goals and objectives must relate back to supporting the vision. Having these clearly understood will be a huge benefit in the requirements elicitation stage, because it will make it easier to prioritize requirements and ensure traceability.

Guidelines

The vision, goals and objectives should not specify the technology to be used. If the vision, goals and objectives focus on the outcomes, benefits and quality to be achieved it will be easier to identify the appropriate technology later, as there could be several options. Goals and objectives to support the vision may come from several sources depending upon the number of business areas impacted.

The reason I have included the section on problem statements before that on scope in this chapter is because the problem statement will help highlight the goals and objectives. A goal is a broad statement highlighting the problem to be addressed. Objectives are more detailed and describe what is going to be done to achieve the goal. It would be very difficult to come up with meaningful and useful goals and objectives without understanding the problems to be addressed. I have seen many projects fail because the vision, goals and objectives have not been understood. If there are project delays because of difficulty eliciting requirements or lots of redirection without anything being delivered, it is likely the scope has not been understood. There is also the risk of the project becoming never ending if the scope is not fixed or broken down enough to make delivering the project feasible within the timeframes set. Vision, goals and objectives are then an enabler for a high-level plan of what needs to be done, who should be involved, high-level estimates and the expected benefits.

Whoever is putting the scope together must also ask and find out about any deadlines and why they are necessary. If there are immovable deadlines associated with the changes required there may need to be priority calls to enable understanding of what should be worked on first to ensure the highest-value benefits are delivered.

EXAMPLE

Google's mission statement is: 'Our mission is to organize the world's information and make it universally accessible and useful.'

The approach by Google is to innovate by looking at the different processes a customer may go through to store information. The statement doesn't solve an issue but sets out the experiences Google wants customers to have. This has enabled Google to come up with a variety of ways to resolve problems customers may have with storing and accessing information. Customers can use Google to conduct internet searches, access and send emails, store their calendar information, look up places to go and visit, store their documentation and much more. Hypothetically, if the mission statement had been more restrictive then the number of solutions on offer to Google would have been much less.

Establishing scope

It is important to take a top-down approach when identifying scope, starting with the top executive involved and working downwards. This is to ensure that the strategic view and direction are captured first, as people lower down in the organization may not be aware of the wider impacts. It also provides the opportunity for all the managers to provide permission to talk to their staff, making the staff's time easier to obtain.

The scope can be captured in different documents depending upon the organization and different roles. Programme managers, project managers, relationship managers, business architects and sometimes business analysts all could have some level of involvement. In terms of documentation the scope could be captured in a project initiation document, vision document, feasibility study or business case, to name just a few.

The scope must be written down to ensure agreement and understanding between all stakeholders. Senior stakeholders may prefer visual stimuli, as a picture can portray lots of information on one page, which is easier and quicker for them to digest. It is also then easier to show other people and to add to and update the scope. It may take several iterations as new objectives to support the goal and vision are uncovered. It may also then be extended with people, systems, processes, products and services.

Once agreed, the scope should be documented in a few paragraphs to summarize the objectives within the scope of the project. It is also important to state what is not in scope. I would advise against having the out-of-scope section looking longer than the in-scope section. Instead relate the out-of-scope section to items that could have been considered but have been discounted owing to project constraints or viability. This could be types or products or services, for example.

CASE STUDY

For the fictional mobile phone retail company Dream Phones I introduced earlier, the CEO has the vision to increase customer sales by 30 per cent. Figure 3.4 demonstrates one method called a vision picture on a page. You can use this approach to display the vision, goals and objectives on one page, which can be built on easily.

In the centre is the vision, which outlines the outcome desired: increase customer sales by 30 per cent. The goals are represented around the outside in the figure, and are sourced from senior stakeholders. The goals contributing to the vision are as follows:

- to make it easier for customers to buy stock;
- to enable targeted marketing messages;
- to predict market trends;
- to enable customers to trade in their old stock for new stock.

There may then be one or more objectives to meet each goal.

The objectives relating to the goal for making it easier for customers to buy stock are to hold stock that customers want to buy and to make the customer journey easier to navigate.

The objectives relating to the goal to enable targeted marketing messages are to improve customer and contact details and to target marketing messages based on customer interest.

The objectives relating to the goal to predict market trends are to understand what customers are ordering, to understand customer interests and to model future growth.

The objective relating to the goal to enable customers to trade in their old stock for new stock is to enable customers to part-exchange old stock for new.

FIGURE 3.4 Vision picture on a page

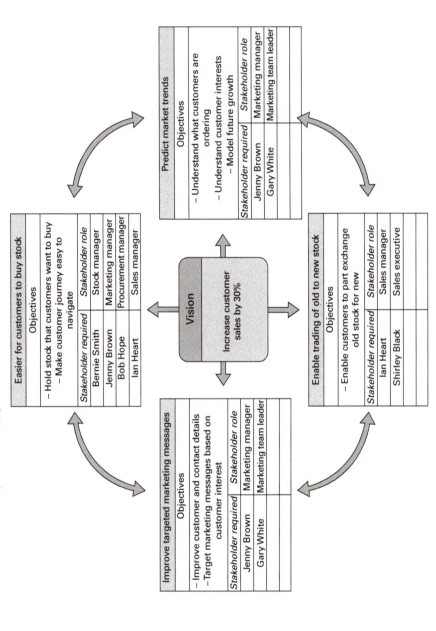

Predict market trends

Objectives	
– Understand what customers are ordering	
– Understand customer interests	
– Model future growth	

Stakeholder required	Stakeholder role
Jenny Brown	Marketing manager
Gary White	Marketing team leader

Easier for customers to buy stock

Objectives	
– Hold stock that customers want to buy	
– Make customer journey easy to navigate	

Stakeholder required	Stakeholder role
Bernie Smith	Stock manager
Jenny Brown	Marketing manager
Bob Hope	Procurement manager
Ian Heart	Sales manager

Vision

Increase customer sales by 30%

Enable trading of old to new stock

Objectives	
– Enable customers to part exchange old stock for new	

Stakeholder required	Stakeholder role
Ian Heart	Sales manager
Shirley Black	Sales executive

Improve targeted marketing messages

Objectives	
– Improve customer and contact details	
– Target marketing messages based on customer interest	

Stakeholder required	Stakeholder role
Jenny Brown	Marketing manager
Gary White	Marketing team leader

SOURCE Reproduced with permission of businessbullet.co.uk, 11 October 2018.

Problem identification techniques covered earlier can also be applied to help identify and analyse the objectives. For example, in problem identification method 2 (process modelling analysis), the case study example in Figure 3.1 started to model the 'as is' end to end process for enabling targeted marketing messages. The conclusions drawn from the analysis were that it was difficult to retrieve the customer and contact details owing to a high dependency on the sales team to provide the information. Another problem identified from looking at the process was that the targeted marketing messages had to be based on the amount of stock available. This starts to illustrate the priority and the size and type of activities needed to meet this objective.

Another example can be illustrated using problem identification method 4 (design thinking). We can apply this to realize the objective relating to targeted marketing messages. Here the example persona of Tony Summers can be utilized to shape the marketing and achieve the overall goal. We know the following:

- Tony wants to update his phone at every opportunity.

- Tony requires plenty of space, good graphics and a high-quality camera for his usage.

- Tony needs the phone to have accurate satellite navigation.

Therefore, to increase sales by 30 per cent in line with the vision of the CEO, one objective would be to use target marketing on a customer who fits Tony Summers's persona. The information from design thinking allows the marketing resources to be focused on an area where arguably it will be most effective. Targeting customers with a different profile, for example those who do not want to update their phone regularly, would likely not complete the goal. This situation demonstrates how business analysis performed correctly can use marketing resources, target the correct customers, save time and meet the sales goal.

___

How do you go about identifying all your stakeholders?

As part of identifying scope it is important to identify the stakeholders who need to be involved. The result of not finding and including all the stakeholders can be that requirements are missed and friction is caused. Ensuring there is agreement between stakeholders as the project progresses will be beneficial in the long term. Full inclusion excludes additional, unknown opinions entering the project at a later date.

All stakeholders need to be identified, along with a knowledge of their business areas and roles. Permission also needs to be granted to speak with them, and it helps if they know they are going to be contacted about the project and have time allocated.

In the example in Figure 3.4, stakeholders are identified. Such an illustration can then evolve as it is shown to all the stakeholders so they can see whether anyone they know about is missing. This then builds on the format that the stakeholders have become familiar with.

Context diagram

One method of identifying stakeholders is using a context diagram. This technique is not concerned with detailing the activities or goals of a project. The project is represented by a circle in the centre of the diagram. People or systems can then be represented around the outside to show a focus on the external interfaces. It enables stakeholders to ascertain easily if there is anyone missing and gives a full picture of the involvement required.

This technique is effective because it helps with understanding the size and complexity of the work involved. The more types of people involved the longer it will take to arrange meetings to understand the different points of

FIGURE 3.5 Context diagram

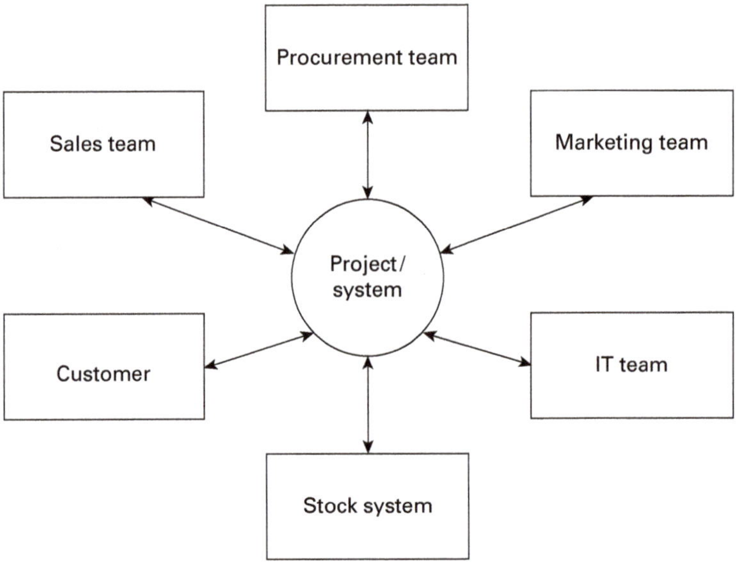

view. The more external systems the more likely the need to understand system constraints and how and what data need to be shared.

How do you identify constraints that might influence the solution?

Constraints are limitations to what options and solutions can be considered. If there are too many constraints, then the options will be so restricted that it could impact the benefits of the changes and make the project less worthwhile. If there aren't enough constraints considered, then understanding what options could be used will be very difficult. It is important not only to identify the constraints but also to establish whether there is any flexibility that can be applied to them and the amount of tolerance that could be allowed. This is important because options could otherwise be discounted that the business would find more beneficial. Hence, it could be willing to compromise on some of the constraints.

There are several different types of constraints. The main project ones often cited are:

- time;
- budget;
- scope;
- quality.

There may be regulatory time constraints or a strong desire from the business to implement the change by a set date. There may be budgetary constraints. Scope itself is a constraint. Quality is also sometimes listed, because if you cannot compromise on time, cost or scope then quality is impacted. Quality constraints can be uncovered by looking at the success criteria for the change and what are known as non-functional requirements (NFRs). NFRs should be investigated early, as they define the quality required, which can impact the options available. NFRs will be covered in more detail in Chapter 6.

There are other constraints that are worth investigating. Some common ones are:

- Resources: These may impact the budget unless more can be added.
- Methodology: Often this is pre-determined outside the control of the project.

- Solution/technology: There may be good reasons why there is a restriction on what can be used. This may be to fit in with enterprise strategy, based on existing technology available or IT policy.

- Contracts: This could be agreements with customers or suppliers that cannot be changed.

- Company policy: This could be around overtime allowed or a restriction on being able to take on contractors, for example. It could also relate to procurement practices or other departmental embedded processes.

- Governance: This could be related to how often and when reporting back is needed on staged gates, who needs to provide authorization of documents and when, or indeed what documentation templates must be used.

- Physical: There could be physical constraints that are limitations, such as meeting rooms or size of rooms.

Investigate the appetite for removing or easing constraints, as this can make a difference to the quality and number of available solutions. Giving the stakeholders some choices may create a more favourable situation. Ask the intention behind each constraint provided to check it really is a constraint. It is important to understand the impact of each constraint identified and to establish whether it can be satisfied in some other way.

EXAMPLE

I had a project where a deadline had been promised to a third party, and I was told this deadline was fixed and had been contractually agreed. In the estimates I had helped to collate it didn't look possible to produce the changes requested to the required deadline. I had to look at other constraints to see what was possible. I looked at whether the scope could be reduced. I was able to gain agreement to increase flexibility in the scope, but nowhere near the amount needed to hit the deadlines. In the end I was able to gain agreement to reduce the quality, which then required a significant amount of manual intervention in correcting so that there was no impact on the end customer. I was able to get this agreement as a short-term measure until a future phase.

How do you identify the needs that might influence the solution?

As you can tell from the previous sections there are lots of different activities to analyse before even trying to document the requirements. A common problem I come across is people writing down the requirements too soon. Requirements are based on changes that need to happen. Changes are desired as a result of problems that need to be overcome or new opportunities that have occurred leading to additional benefits. The scope will vary depending upon where the biggest benefits can be obtained, the costs involved and the constraints. These are all reasons why the first activity should not be to write down requirements but to understand the context of the change, problems, opportunities and scope first. This will also ensure traceability to make sure needs relate back, as if they do not then they should not fall within the scope of the project. Equally if there is a problem with no requirements relating to it then there is something missing.

Requirements are covered in much more detail in Chapter 5. I've mentioned them here because sometimes there is a need to size a project and understand the solutions before deciding whether it should in fact be a project. It can be useful to categorize the needs and any constraints that might influence or restrict the solutions. Some companies will want to go into more detail with the requirements because they will want to have a more accurate estimate or will wait until after the full business requirements before dealing with the business case. At the moment we are assuming that it is just a shorter investigation required to understand quickly whether the project is worth doing without spending too much money on it.

The rest of this section considers needs that you might want to include. They should be kept fairly high-level and time-boxed to a small number of days. Otherwise you may be duplicating work later when it becomes a project. You may want to add to this when appropriate. Remember the purpose of this stage is just to capture enough about the change to understand the solution options and to size the change to identify whether it is worth doing.

Regulatory

Any regulatory impacts need to be summarized. This makes it clear what is compulsory and requires a solution. For example, this could be changes to company policy, authorization, principles, new rules, treating customers fairly, record keeping and many others.

Controls

An understanding is required of what controls must be in place. This could relate to communication, staff or controls around processes or calculations, for instance.

Business processes

It is useful to understand the business processes impacted. This will help ascertain the size of the project. We identified the number of stakeholders previously; however, the number of processes will also be a good indicator of the size and complexity of the project.

Communications with customers

Communications such as letters and documents are a useful indicator as to the size of a project. If at this stage the number is not known, then assumptions can be stated for future validation and the types of changes can be listed.

Management information (MI) and reporting

This is to bring out whether the solution needs to incorporate any MI or reporting. At a high level this should establish what types of reports are needed and for whom.

Organizational structure

Any organizational changes need to be specified. For example, if there are new processes then there may need to be additional skills not currently available.

Data

Confirmation is needed of whether there are any changes required to existing data or whether new data are needed that are not currently collected or stored. The categories of data, such as customer or product, could be specified.

Strategic planning

It needs to be established whether any strategic planning is required and whether any solution must be in line with the strategic business direction.

Product or service

It needs to be identified whether there are any product or service changes required.

Learning and development

Is it envisaged that new training materials will be required or new training needs rolled out?

Timelines

It needs to be established whether there are any timelines that must be met, and the importance of meeting deadlines, including why, needs to be stated.

How do you ensure the overall solution agreed will meet the business needs?

Once the problems, opportunities, scope, external interfaces and constraints are understood, the types of solutions can be identified. Solutions can vary from fully automated systems to lots of manual workarounds and processes. There may also be decisions to be made on whether to build in-house, extend current systems, buy an off the shelf package or outsource, for example. There should always be more than one solution considered in order to understand the appetite for the changes and the budget. Each solution considered should have either a strengths, weaknesses, opportunities and threats (SWOT) analysis conducted or pros and cons listed. If going for the pros and cons approach, make sure you list the recommendation first and do include both pros and cons. I've seen so many people miss out the cons for their preferred solution. I've never come across a solution without some cons to it.

To generate many possible solutions, analyse the problems identified and brainstorm with different stakeholders to obtain different perspectives and experiences. Examine, compare and probe each one. Questions to ask are:

- What should we do?
- Where in the process should it be done?
- When should we do it?
- Who should do it?
- How should it be done?

Innovation triggers can be used to generate solutions. Look at other domains. There may be lessons that can be learnt from unrelated industries. They may have similar problems but have adopted different solutions. If you can get direct customer participation, then this may also help generate new solutions. Looking at different perspectives to improve an experience may be useful, for example new ways to get information to customers that they will value, adding convenience, providing a service faster or looking at what customers may value.

Not all solutions are IT system related. IT may be only part of the solution. Identifying solutions may therefore require enterprise architects, solution architects, data architects, business owners and others to discuss the pros, cons and appetite for each type of solution. A common problem I come across is where IT stakeholders assume that the solution can be dealt with manually if difficult but no one gains the business's buy-in or understanding of this. It can then sometimes end up with the project being completed and the business then finding parts of what it was expecting missing, not having realized the onus was on it to come up with an answer.

Therefore, solutions listed should correlate with all areas expected. Some of the solution types could be system changes, letters, processes, data, data cleansing, MI and reporting, business areas, governance, compliance, legal and training. These could vary depending upon the industry you are in. It is worth exploring all the types of solutions required to gain an understanding of the overall picture. This will also help with understanding the size of the project and estimating all the costs involved. There is no point just sizing the IT solution if the headcount to support additional manual processes massively increases and isn't acceptable to the business.

Pros may include alignment to the strategic view, meeting timelines, being within budget, meeting all the needs, being automated, resolving other issues and having the capacity to be reapplied.

Cons may include being a tactical option, taking longer to implement, having more manual processes and being over budget.

How do you justify the benefits and estimated costs?

An impact assessment is required to allow understanding of whether the recommended solution is worth doing. A comparison is required between the benefits and the costs. If the reason for the change is that it is required by regulation, then there may not be many benefits, but the change will still be obligatory. If the change is more for commercial reasons, then the average payback period accepted by senior management as worthwhile is three to five years as a guide. The costs and benefits should be revisited throughout a project in case the original estimates and assumptions prove to be incorrect. As each project progresses it should be easier to obtain more accurate estimates.

Estimation

ESTIMATION TECHNIQUES

There are several estimation techniques and methods that can be used. The method used will depend upon the level of certainty required and contingency expected.

The most basic is T-shirt sizing, where the key people have a meeting together and decide whether it is a small change, small project, medium project, large project or very large project.

Another method is to have a cost range, for example under £50,000, £50,000–£100,000, £100,000–£500,000, £500,000–£1 million and over £1 million. This range will vary depending upon the size of your company and the typical size of projects implemented.

Three-point estimation involves providing three figures: a worst-case scenario cost, a likely cost and an optimistic cost.

CONFIDENCE

Individuals may be requested to provide estimates for their areas based on the understanding that they will be expected to be out by a maximum plus or minus percentage. This needs to be a reasonable amount based on the amount of detail given. Based on the early stages described in this chapter of identifying the problems to be solved, stakeholders, goals, objectives, scope, needs and possible high-level solutions, the best practice is 100 per cent contingency either way. This really requires a discipline of ensuring that the stakeholders estimating are not adding their own contingency on top. As a rule of thumb the work can be re-estimated within 25–50 per cent either way once the business requirements document is written and within 15 per cent once the solutions design document is complete. It really depends upon how much senior managers feel they need to know before spending money on a project and how long they are prepared to wait before they can decide.

TYPES OF COSTS

There will be different types of costs to collate. You will need to separate out development costs from running costs after the solution is implemented. The first cost category to consider is people: who will be required to make the change happen and how many days' effort will be required from each, which will allow their day rates to be calculated. The same will be required for running costs if additional people are required as a result. Hardware and software costs will need to be collated, including any consultancy and licence costs. Third parties may need to be contacted for these figures. Because it is pre-project work, they will often provide their services free of charge, and talking to them will provide an indication of how keen they are. Include any location costs there may be, and establish whether there will be any costs to add on top for funding the change.

ASSUMPTIONS

You will need to make sure assumptions are clearly stated regardless of what impact estimation approach is used. Assumptions will show what the estimates are based on. If any of them prove incorrect then the estimate will need to be revisited. The more assumptions that can be validated the more confidence there will be in the estimates. The same applies to the benefits.

DIFFERENCES BETWEEN WATERFALL AND AGILE

In waterfall projects, estimates tend to get revisited at each stage of the project as more detail is known. In agile there is still a need to estimate the time required to implement the whole project, as resources and budget still need to be planned as they are for waterfall-based projects. However, estimation is continual rather than at the end of each stage. There are additional estimation techniques used. In agile the different stages of the project are broken down into chunks and worked on iteratively and incrementally. To start with, a backlog is created of the features required for the solution. This is fairly high-level, as the detail behind each feature is worked on incrementally depending upon order of priority. Priority is judged based on the value it brings, with the features providing the highest value delivered first. The benefit of this is that if the project estimates were wrong and the project runs out of money then something has been delivered, which is the features of the highest value. If the money runs out for a waterfall project then nothing may have been delivered.

Benefits

Benefits are important to help ensure the work required to implement the change is worthwhile. There are two types of benefits:

1 Quantitative.
    - These benefits can be quantified. They could be direct reduced costs because of the solution being implemented. This could be because of savings due to changes in hardware, software, people and processes, for example.
    - There may be indirect savings because of the solution. There could also be costs avoided as a result of the changes being implemented. Even regulatory changes will have benefits associated in terms of the costs of fines avoided.
2 Qualitative.
    - Not all benefits can be quantified. These tend to be known as intangible benefits or qualitative benefits. This means a cost cannot be associated with them. They can still provide a good reason for going ahead with a change. Examples are reputational risk reduced, staff morale improved and customer experience improved.

04

Business context and business processes

Introduction

In Chapter 3, we covered how companies may instigate process modelling prior to initiating a project to help them understand the problems and the amount of change required.

This chapter introduces several other benefits and reasons for using process modelling and how to apply these different techniques in different ways. To keep things simple, I am only going to cover flowcharts for high-level process diagrams and Business Process Model and Notation (BPMN) to show more detail around processes. I will also cover a limited number of symbols that will be applicable to most of the scenarios you will be interested in.

Questions covered in this chapter around business processes

This chapter answers the following questions:

- What is process modelling?
- How do you work out what level of detail to use for mapping processes?
- What are the benefits of process modelling?
- How do you go about identifying the processes in the first place?
- How do you put a process map together?
- What standard and symbols should you use?
- How do you analyse process maps for improvement?

What is process modelling?

Process modelling is a way to visually show what happens in an organization or department, or the route to achieving a goal to ensure a common understanding, allow analysis and identify improvements. A visual representation is much easier to put together and analyse than the amount of narrative it would take to describe often complex projects. It also makes it clearer to see where information has not been captured to present the full picture. Analysis can then be undertaken using process modelling to plan out improvements and what needs to change to get to the desired state.

A series of standardized symbols are used to represent what goes on within a process. The diagrams should be easy to understand for anyone who looks at them. A key can also be provided to help the audience understand the different symbols used.

How do you work out what level of detail to use for mapping processes?

Processes can be modelled to provide different levels of information and be used for different purposes. Each of the processes can then be broken down further to provide another lower level of information.

High-level processes

High-level processes focus on the primary activities end to end. This is useful for understanding the context and what is involved. The process steps should ideally fit on a single side of A4 paper in landscape and number no more than 6–10 steps. A high-level diagram will not include the low-level task decisions made or alternative flows. Symbols used in the diagram are limited to a simple process flow showing just the primary grouped activities and the sequence.

Lower-level processes

Each time a process is broken down, more detail is provided for the process. The activities in each process and the decisions can be shown for each business area/team or role involved.

Process modelling can go into lower levels of detail to show alternative activities that may happen that have a different result without achieving the end goal. The main activities that achieve the end goal most of the time are known as the 'main success path' or 'happy path'. Activities that deviate from the goal or require other decisions to be made before achieving the end goal are called 'alternative paths'.

What are the benefits of process modelling?

Scope

Process modelling helps with understanding the scope of a project. Once the end to end processes are understood, the tasks relating to any changes required can be broken down further. Therefore process modelling is worth doing in the early stages of a project.

Requirements

Stakeholders are more likely to be familiar with and understand their processes as opposed to their requirements. Asking stakeholders to describe their processes is often a more productive and easier conversation to have initially. The role of the business analyst is to help the stakeholders to understand their requirements through their processes, and process modelling is an important technique to help achieve that. It also helps to group the requirements drawn from these discussions to avoid the risks of duplication and to improve readability.

Improvements

An additional benefit of process modelling is that there are techniques such as BPMN that can provide lots of further information. BPMN can be used to show which processes are manual, which are automated, which involve user interaction with computer systems and which involve interactions between different stakeholder roles and teams. This means improvements can be looked for in a process and hence requirements built on an improved process rather than an inefficient one.

Whole end to end picture

If an end to end process goes across several teams the stakeholders will likely only know their own area. This makes eliciting requirements difficult without seeing the whole end to end picture first. Providing this end to end visual picture helps all the stakeholders to see not just their own processes but the processes of others. This may then uncover further requirements that would not have been apparent otherwise. Once stakeholders can visually see their own processes in front of them it will often help them see gaps and processes missing that they would not have thought of otherwise when explaining what they do. It will also show if teams are duplicating work, conducting unnecessary handoffs or inadvertently causing problems later in the process.

Scenarios

One of the most common mistakes I have come across is there being too much focus on a main scenario. Process modelling will make it easier to have discussions on what alternative scenarios need to take place. Any solution will need to consider alternatives, as otherwise there is a risk the process will fall over or be of limited use.

Knowledge sharing

Process modelling is an effective technique for brand new processes to enable the business to understand what changes to expect and prepare for. There is a benefit too in using processing modelling to document existing processes, which can help with ensuring that the different stakeholders are working consistently and for newcomers to the company. Updating process modelling is also relatively easy compared to trawling through text.

Target operating model

The target operating model will be covered in Chapter 8. Process modelling is a key part in putting together a target operating model, because conversations will need to be based on the processes and the skills and number of employees required to support them.

How do you go about identifying the processes in the first place?

The method of identifying what the processes are before modelling them is to understand the triggers and goals. A trigger is the event that instigates

TABLE 4.1 Identifying business processes

Trigger	Goal
Customer decides to book a holiday	Book a holiday
Customer registers an account	Register an account
A customer complaint is received	Handle complaints received
Home insurance up for renewal in one month	Renew home insurance
Application received for a new bank account	Open a new bank account
Customer visits the company website	Customer is requested to respond to a customer satisfaction survey
Every 15th day of the month	To send out bank statements to customers monthly
One month before an existing insurance policy needs renewing	Send out insurance renewal notices

the process. A goal is what needs to be achieved as an outcome of the process. See Table 4.1 for some examples.

You can then work out how many processes there are depending upon the number of triggers and goals. This should form part of an initial meeting with stakeholders prior to running more detailed workshops. The objective of this initial meeting is to understand the goals, triggers and stakeholders involved with each. For each of the triggers it is worth clarifying whether the process is triggered by a person or by time. The examples in Table 4.1 relating to the 15th of the month and one month before an existing insurance policy needs renewing are examples of time-related triggers.

The number of workshops required and estimated effort can be determined based on the number of processes identified. The number of people to invite will depend on how many different people are involved with the process. It is common for people to know only their part of the process, so if you need to understand the end to end flow of a process then you need to ensure there is a representative for each area invited. You also need to think how many processes can be covered in a single session. I would suggest that you plan in a minimum number of two to three workshops per process, as I have always found that stakeholders are more likely to spot missing alternative flows or tasks when reviewing, because they will automatically do tasks without realizing.

How do you put a process map together?

When preparing for a process modelling workshop there are two main recommended approaches. They both involve building the diagrams in the workshop. I would not recommend writing down lots of notes and doing the diagrams afterwards. This will not bring out as many benefits as a visual picture being built in front of a stakeholder's eyes, as it is this that often instigates the stakeholder to see what is missing and slows the pace down to ensure nothing is missed.

The first method is to take a big roll of brown paper in and lots of sticky notes. Put the brown paper on the wall in advance of the attendees turning up. With the attendees present, draw horizontal lines to form what are known as swim lanes. The swim lanes are to represent the different teams or roles of people who are involved with the process. Agree what these are and how many are required. Give out the sticky notes for the attendees to write out their tasks for the most popular scenario. All attendees must agree to the same scenario. The benefit of the sticky notes approach is that stakeholders will frequently think of additional tasks they may have forgotten. It is then much easier to move the sticky notes around as discussion progresses.

TIP

I tend to take some sticky tape with me to ensure the sticky notes do not fall off when people are happy with their positioning. I've recently discovered super-sticky notes. Alternatively spray adhesive works well, as does taking photos on your mobile phone.

Once the stickies are on the wall, in order and in swim lanes, discuss whether there are any processes missing that go in between swim lanes. Whenever there is a handoff from one swim lane to another, identify the send and receive tasks. The next step is to walk through each task in the process and identify whether there are any alternative scenarios. This may involve adding in decisions (represented by diamonds) and identifying tasks that can be done in parallel. Do not worry about syntax yet, as we will cover that in the next section. See Figure 4.1 illustrating the process described above at a high level.

FIGURE 4.1 High-level business process model

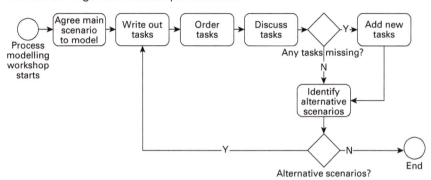

The second method is to use diagramming software like Enterprise Architect or Visio. This has the benefit of not having to type up the work electronically afterwards, as you are doing it in the meeting, thus saving time. To do this you will have to feel very confident with the software and have an appropriate-sized screen. I tend to use this only if I have a smart screen, because it is then easier to move the tasks around. Putting the processes together is then the same as in the first method.

You can catch additional information by adding data inputs or outputs, related documentation or systems to a task. Tasks can be identified as to whether they are manual, require interaction between a user and a system or a task needs to be fully automated. If looking to improve a process you could also ask how long each task takes.

You will want to understand the 'as is' processes first if you need to understand what the problems are for the existing situation, and it may be required before you can understand the 'to be' process. The 'to be' processes are useful prior to documenting requirements, because you will want to build requirements on the 'to be' process. It can also be used to demonstrate and get buy-in from the business on understanding the amount of changes that need to happen.

It is good practice to get the processes signed off before moving on to documenting the requirements. They are so closely linked, and this will reduce the number of changes to the requirements document.

What standard and symbols should you use?

The standard is BPMN for documenting lower-level processes. There are other notations and process flows you can use, but why not use a standard framework that is industry recognized and reused all over the world? It then makes your skills very cross-transferable if you understand and use it. BPMN is managed by the Object Management Group (OMG), which owns its development and releases new versions. Even though it is a standard framework there are still several different symbols that mean the same thing and different methods for using them. I'm going to cover some of the main symbols using the notation from version 2.0 and what I believe to be the most widely applicable method (see https://www.omg.org/spec/BPMN/2.0/). BPMN has more than 50 symbols, but it is recommended you restrict the number you use to what is most appropriate for your situation. The ones I'm introducing you to will probably meet your needs for most of the time. It is important to agree up front which symbols and method you are going to use at your company or for your project. This may already be defined.

Some people worry about whether stakeholders who haven't come across BPMN before will understand it. It is very intuitive, so the chances are they will get it. In illustration of this, a BPMN process diagram was included as Figure 3.1 in Chapter 3 without explanation of the notation at that stage. I would suggest you still include a legend key to explain each of the symbols as part of your documentation.

The different types of symbols can be split into the following categories:

- events;
- participants;
- activities;
- gateways;
- connecting objects;
- data.

See Figure 4.2, which shows the main symbols and provides a legend key.

Activities can also be amended in BPMN version 2.0 to show whether activities are manual, activities require interaction between a user and a system or a task needs to be fully automated. These are represented by different symbols in the corner of the activity shape (see Figure 4.3). Their use is demonstrated in Figure 4.4 in the case study on page 89.

FIGURE 4.2 BPMN symbols

Symbol	Name	Description
Events		
Start	Start event	Symbolizes the start of a process. You can add the word 'start' or what the trigger is as a narrative or leave it blank.
End	End event	Shows the end of the process. You can add the word 'end' or the result of the process or leave it blank. There could be more than one end event in a process if there is more than one outcome.
Participants		
Company A / Sales / IT	Pool and swim lanes	A pool is represented by Company A in the illustration example. It should always accompany one or more swim lanes. It will generally be used to represent different boundaries such as company level in a process or swim lanes belonging in different boundaries. A swim lane shows the different participants typically being used to show activities carried out by different departments or roles.
Activities		
	Activity	Represents each activity carried out as part of a process. The naming convention for activities should be short and consist of a verb and an object.
+	Collapsed sub-process	If you wish to show that an activity has been broken down further in a separate process diagram, then the plus symbol can be used.
Connecting objects		
⟶	Sequence flow	Shows sequence and helps in navigating through the process and knowing what order to follow.
o‑ ‑ ‑ ‑ ‑ ‑ ▷	Message flow	The sequence flow is not used when showing the relationship between two tasks in different pools. Instead the message flow symbol is used.
Gateways		
◇	XOR gateway	Represents a decision or more than one option that applies before proceeding to the next task. A question is often asked in conjunction with this symbol being used, and it will have a minimum of two sequence flows going out of it with the different options possible.
Data		
	Data store with association symbol	This can be used to show which tasks use a system or have data stored centrally. The association symbol represented by the dotted line attaches to the relevant tasks. The data store can be named to show the system that the stakeholders are familiar with.
	Data object	This can be used to show which tasks can be associated with different types of documentation. It could be a report, form, guide etc. The association symbol represented by the dotted line attaches to the relevant tasks. The data object can be named with the documentation that the stakeholders are familiar with.

FIGURE 4.3 Additional BPMN symbols supported by version 2.0

Symbol	Name	Description
  ✉ (shaded envelope icon) / ✉ (unshaded envelope icon)	Activity with a throwing or receiving message event symbol	The shaded envelope represents a send communication. The unshaded envelope represents a receive communication. They come as a pair. Wherever you have a send message you will have a corresponding receive one. These are normally used when activities go from one swim lane to another to show the handoffs.
 (person icon)	Activity that shows a user using a system	A little person symbol shows which activities involve a user using a system to complete it.
 (cogs icon)	Activity that is automated by software	Two little cogs represent an automated system activity.
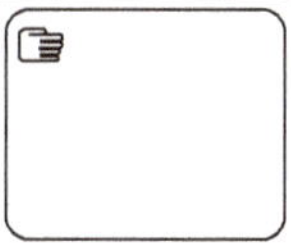 (hand icon)	Activity that is manual and carried out by a human	A little hand symbol represents manual activities.

CASE STUDY

Let's now build on the example shown in Chapter 3 with Figure 3.1, which documented the processes to send out targeted marketing messages for selling Dream Phones' mobile phones. Figure 4.4 develops this with a few additions that were made after a review with the business in which one of the stakeholders realized that, owing to new regulation, the business could send out marketing material only if the customer had given consent. More detail was also provided on how the marketing team decided what to promote. It was decided to show the breakdown of this in a lower-level process diagram. The process diagram in Figure 4.4 has now been updated to reflect these changes.

See Figures 4.2 and 4.3 for the key to describing these symbols.

The swim lanes represent either the business areas or the roles involved with the process. They are drawn first. The swim lanes in Figure 4.4 are Marketing, Sales, Procurement and Customer. Swim lanes should always have a notation called a pool around them. In this instance the pools are labelled Dream Phones, which is the name of the fictional company, and Customer.

FIGURE 4.4 Updated process diagram from Figure 3.1

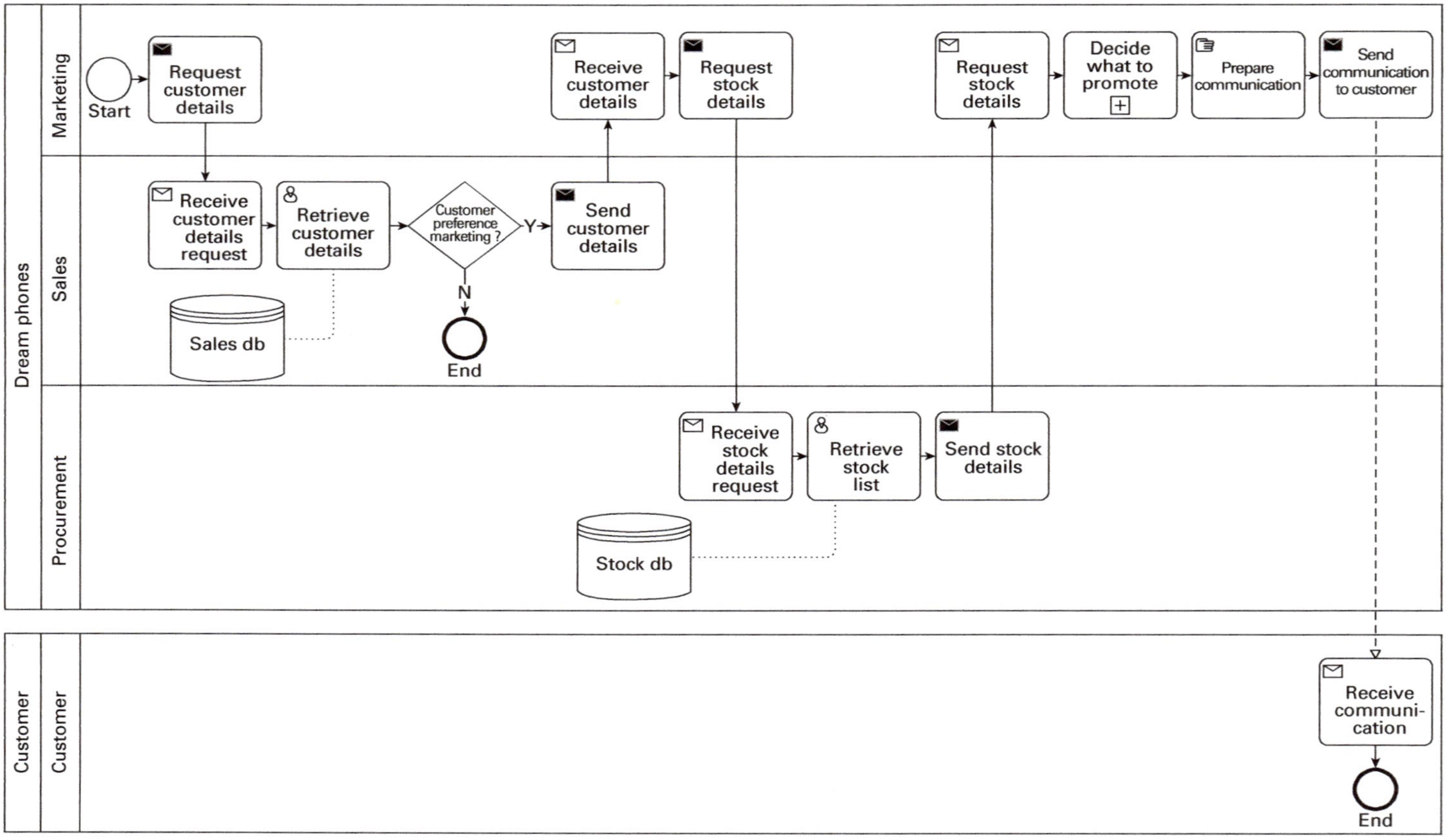

Each process has a start and an end event, which are labelled in Figure 4.4 as 'Start' and 'End'. The end event has a thicker circle, which represents the end of the process. There are now two end events.

Each activity is represented by a rectangular box. The naming convention for activities should be short and consist of a verb and an object, for example, from Figure 4.4, 'Request customer details'.

An activity can be assigned an activity type and represented with a symbol in the top left-hand corner. This is useful when using processes to identify requirements, because it provides more detail about the requirements. The shaded envelope represents a send communication. The unshaded envelope represents a receive communication. Wherever you have a send message you will have a corresponding receive one. These are normally used when tasks go from one swim lane to another to show the handoffs. A little person symbol such as the one shown in the 'Retrieve customer details' and 'Retrieve stock list' tasks represents a user using a system. A little hand symbol such as the one shown in the 'Prepare communication' task represents the task being manual. I haven't used it in Figure 4.4, but another common symbol you might want to use is a cog symbol. This represents a service task performed by software.

If a plus sign is shown, for example in a rectangular box, then this illustrates there is another process that exists that breaks down the tasks further. This is represented in the 'Decide what to promote' rectangular box in Figure 4.4.

Sequence flows that show the flow order of tasks are represented with arrows.

A decision is represented with a diamond shape. In the Dream Phones case, the sales team checks, for each customer, whether there is a customer preference that allows marketing. If the answer is no, the team cannot send those customer details to marketing and the process for that customer ends. If the decision is yes, then those customer details can be sent to marketing.

When the sales team retrieves customer details or the procurement team retrieves stock, it interacts with a data store. This is represented in Figure 4.4 by the symbols shown as 'Sales db' and 'Stock db'.

You may have noticed that the dotted arrow symbol on the far right looks different to a sequence flow. This symbol is called a message flow and is used whenever showing activities from one pool to another.

How do you analyse process maps for improvement?

Identifying value

A good first step for finding improvements is to analyse your 'as is' process map to understand what changes are required to create an improved 'to be' process.

Start with questioning each activity identified in the process. Identify whether it adds value to the product or service and whether the end customer would notice if it was removed. You will be surprised at how often activities are done because they have always been done that way or because people have added additional controls as they didn't trust the process. I was once told about a process that involved adding a red dot to a document. This carried on for years without anyone understanding why. After much investigation it was discovered that it was introduced by a staff member who had left years before and used it to signify when it was time to meet up for a coffee with another staff member who received the document further on in the process. Subsequent staff members started to add red dots because they thought it was required. If value isn't added by an activity in a process, challenge whether it is required.

Identifying existing problems

It is equally important to get the stakeholders involved to identify which of the activities in the processes cause them problems. This will help enable understanding of what further changes may be required and whether they can be simplified. Discuss and identify problems relating to time lags and highlight significant ones on the process diagram. Question whether it is possible to remove these delays and the impact it would have. Delay is likely to happen where there are heavy dependencies on manual processes if a backlog builds up or if a process is quite resource-intensive. It may also happen if there are multiple handoffs, as time can be taken up by waiting for responses from other areas. Question whether all the handoffs are necessary, as each time there is a handoff there is a risk of communication breaking down. Establish whether any areas of rework can be reduced and the volumes that can occur. Find out why the problem occurs and whether anything can be done to reduce or eliminate it.

Inspecting decisions

Inspect the decisions that are made throughout the process, especially if they are related to manual intervention. Challenge each one as to whether it is necessary. For example, if it is there to handle errors then consider whether there could be activities introduced earlier on that would make the error handling redundant.

Reviewing data objects

Where data objects are shown as a document, form or report feeding into or out of an activity, question whether they are required or whether there are any changes that could lead to improvements.

Checking logical flow

Finally check the whole process and identify whether it flows logically and in the right order. Investigate whether any activities could be done in parallel to reduce the end to end processing time. The results of this analysis will feed into your problem statement, success criteria, requirements and business readiness preparations.

05

Business context/understanding requirements

Introduction

We covered in Chapter 3 the importance of understanding scope, problems, goals and objectives. This is normally the first level to be addressed where a top-down approach to requirements is used. The hierarchy for defining requirements and this logical order should be adhered to regardless of the methodology used (see Figure 5.1). This chapter focuses on defining the business requirements, which is the second level down in the hierarchy. These often get fed into a business requirements document as an artefact. Each level down produces greater levels of detail. By the end of this chapter you will understand the importance of the hierarchy of requirements and be equipped with the ability not to mix the levels up by knowing that they have different purposes and audiences. The first level is aimed more at senior managers to ensure that their vision and the problem are understood correctly. The second level, which is business requirements, is aimed at the business stakeholders to ensure that what they want is understood. The third level is the solution requirements level, which investigates how the requirements are to be met and aimed at the stakeholders who need to deliver them. In some circumstances a bottom-up approach is used, where the hierarchy described above is carried out in reverse. This is not as common and normally to cover circumstances where a product is being reverse-engineered.

The term 'requirement elicitation' has been used throughout rather than 'requirement gathering', because it is the business analyst's role to elicit what is required. There are techniques to help the stakeholders understand their requirements. It is not about sitting with a blank piece of paper and asking what stakeholders want, as often this will not return reflective requirements. This chapter will therefore cover some of the elicitation techniques that will help you.

Formulating a good requirement is as important as being able to find out what is required. It is difficult to write requirements without making assumptions or being ambiguous. Therefore, we will cover how to avoid this and some tips for recognizing when this happens. We will then cover what goes into a typical business requirements document. This will help you to write one and provide a solid foundation for the rest of the project.

Business requirements, assumptions, dependencies, risks and issues are all included in a business requirements document. Mixing these up will have huge implications. For example, if you list a requirement as an assumption, there is a risk it will not get picked up as a change to be made. We will therefore define what each of these is in order to help ensure it is categorized correctly and look at some of the implications of mixing them up.

Questions covered in this chapter for understanding business requirements

- Why is there a hierarchy of requirements and why does it matter?
- What are the different methods for requirements elicitation?
- How do you formulate a good requirement?
- What goes into a business requirements document?
- What are assumptions, dependencies, risks and issues?
- What are the implications of mixing up business requirements, assumptions, dependencies, risks and issues?

Why is there a hierarchy of requirements and why does it matter?

Effective business analysis includes specifying requirements at different levels and being able to conduct traceability to ensure throughout the development that each level of the requirements is being met. It is important to understand the difference between the levels of the hierarchy of requirements and not to mix them up.

Understanding the problems, scope, goals and objectives is the first step of the hierarchy, and this outlines the business need. This is followed by the second level, which is eliciting the business requirements. This sets out what is required to meet the business need from the stakeholder's point of view. The third level provides more detail and sets out how the stakeholder wants the solutions to work from a behaviour point of view and their characteristics.

FIGURE 5.1 Requirements hierarchy

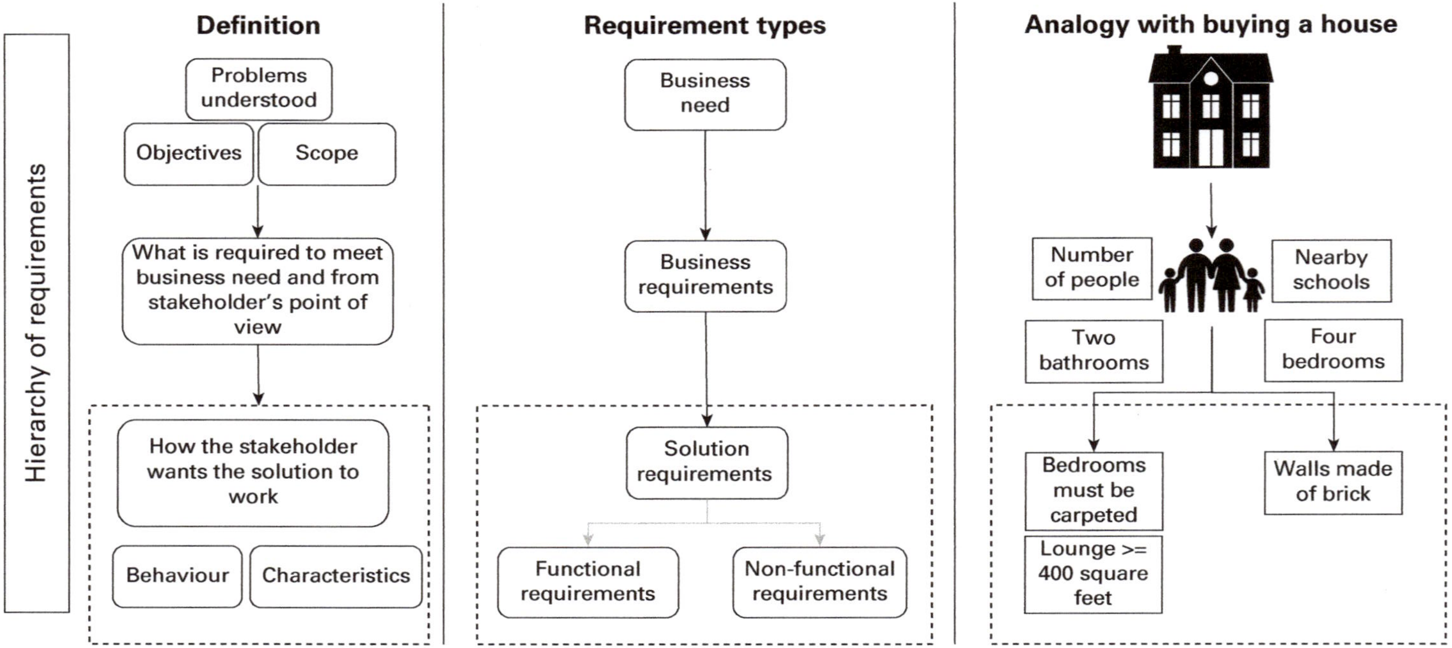

Definition

Problems understood

Objectives | Scope

What is required to meet business need and from stakeholder's point of view

How the stakeholder wants the solution to work

Behaviour | Characteristics

Hierarchy of requirements

Requirement types

Business need

Business requirements

Solution requirements

Functional requirements | Non-functional requirements

Analogy with buying a house

Number of people | Nearby schools

Two bathrooms | Four bedrooms

Bedrooms must be carpeted | Walls made of brick

Lounge >= 400 square feet

Business need

Establishing the problems, scope, goals and objects of a project first allows for the breadth of the changes being proposed to be determined. In doing so the business need is outlined. The business need provides detail about how much a project might cost compared to the expected benefits as well as the resources required and engagement needed. This is at a high level and offers an overview to enable understanding of what is required to meet the objectives or how to address the changes required. It provides only enough information to decide whether it is worth making the change without spending too much time on going into lots of detail. A business need will outline the objective, for example to buy a house to be closer to a new workplace, but will not provide any more detail than that. If decision makers agree that the estimations based on the overview make it likely that the project is worth doing, then the next level in the hierarchy is to set out the business requirements.

Business requirements

The next step in the hierarchy is to define the business requirements. Business requirements are written from the point of view of stakeholders focusing on what they want in relation to the objectives specified in the business need. Requirements are fed into a business requirements document (BRD) as an artefact, which, if a detailed business case is required, will be incorporated as part of the business case. There should be no reference to how the requirements should be met in this document, just what they are. Continuing the analogy of buying a house used in the previous subsection, the house is the objective. The high-level business requirements for this could be as follows:

- The house must accommodate two adults and two children.
- The house must be able to be lived in for the next seven years.
- The house must be located within the catchment area of good schools.
- The house must be within one-hour commuting distance of the new workplace.

Lower-level business requirements then go into more detail from each stakeholder's point of view, such as needing four bedrooms and two bathrooms. The BRD should avoid solutions for how each requirement may be met, as there are so many possibilities that could be considered. Requirements are stable and less likely to change, whereas solutions can change. One of the mistakes I often come across is the addition of solutions to the business requirements document, which then has to be completely rewritten each time a different solution is considered.

Solution requirements

The next level down in the requirements hierarchy is what is known as solution requirements. In instances where IT systems are involved, these requirements may also be called system requirements. Solution requirements focus on how the business requirements can be met. They provide the level of detail to be able to deliver the solution. In some instances an IT architect or other field expert may need to be involved with the help of a business analyst to understand and gain consensus on the best solution to take forward.

Solution requirements can be further broken down into functional and non-functional requirements. Chapter 6 will focus more on the techniques to help identify functional and non-functional requirements. An example of a functional requirement, using the house analogy, is that the house must have a lounge that is greater than 400 square feet so that the family sofa can fit into it. Functional requirements relate to the functionality of the product. If the person delivering the solution didn't have this level of detail the users could end up with something they didn't want. Non-functional requirements relate to the quality of the product. This may refer, for example, to what materials are required.

CASE STUDY

Going back to the case study of the fictional firm Dream Phones from previous chapters, let us consider an example of the requirements at each level of the hierarchy.

Business need level

- To enable customers to part-exchange old stock for new.

Business requirements level

- To enable customers to provide their old phone details, including the make, model number, condition, original provider of the phone and contract end date.
- To quote to customers how much the second-hand mobile phones are worth based on the information received.

- To enable customers to return their old mobile phones.
- To enable customers to provide details of the new phone they require, including the make, model number, colour and capacity.
- To enable customers to provide customer and payment details.
- To receive the old mobile phones and provide the new ones requested.
- To recycle old mobile phones received.

Solution requirements level – functional

- Customers need to be able to request a quote for their old mobile phone via a new web page on the company's website.
- Customers need to be able to register or log on to the company's website.

Solution requirements level – non-functional

- The company's website should have a response time of no more than 5 seconds.

What are the different methods for requirements elicitation?

There are various methods for eliciting requirements, and it is up to you as the business analyst to pick the most appropriate for the situation. I have already covered process modelling, which is a good foundation for understanding the business requirements. Using each of the processes in the 'to be' process model you can start to define each business requirement. It is important to define the 'to be' processes prior to writing the business requirements. This gives you and your stakeholders a chance to improve the processes first and to understand what teams or roles are to be involved for each process after the changes have been made. It is useful to annotate the process model to show which activities are new, which are modified and which have no changes. It is also helpful to align the requirements to each of the new and modified business process steps to ensure that the requirements support the execution of the business process. This also provides a good framework for helping the stakeholders understand the logical flow of the requirements. Details around business process modelling are set out in Chapter 4, and it can be a useful technique at other stages of a project too.

The following subsections discuss other complementary approaches that you may use in addition to or as part of mapping the business processes.

Interviews

One method is to conduct interviews with individual stakeholders or organize workshops for grouped discussions. See Chapter 2 for guidance on facilitating meetings and workshops.

It makes sense to think about the questions you want to ask your stakeholder attendees in advance. However, if they appear prepared with material to show you that still fits with the agenda, be open to letting them walk you through that instead.

It is good practice to send out minutes, actions and decisions after each interview. This provides the opportunity for the interviewee(s) to add any further information, make alterations or make sure there is the same understanding. The actions and decisions can then also be tracked and chased up to ensure actions are carried out and decisions understood.

Documentation

Reviewing existing documentation is another useful method. This could reveal existing processes, inputs or outputs. Ask for copies to be sent to you and check how up to date and accurate these are. This may also help you to understand what information is required as part of the business requirements, especially if forms and reports can be provided.

Surveys

Surveys could be another method if there are many stakeholders to obtain knowledge from. There are so many free survey tools available these days, and they can be customized as necessary. Surveys are useful too if there are a large number of stakeholders who are not easily accessible. Surveys can be a good method to help identify stakeholders, as they can be sent out to a large network of people. A disadvantage of surveys is that the questions are defined in advance and, if they are worded incorrectly, you cannot drill down into more detail easily. If you think you might need more detail as a result of the survey, make sure you obtain contact details of the respondents in case you need to go back with more questions individually.

Observation

It also might be worth considering observation. This has the benefit of allowing you to work out what is happening and the different scenarios. Observation could provide additional information that the stakeholder might not have thought to mention, as it has become routine or commonplace. This will also give a sense of what difficulties may occur and provide context. A word of warning, though, is to be aware that stakeholders' behaviour will alter if they know they are being watched. It is important to make sure stakeholders feel at ease, and it will be useful if you can get them to give you some narrative of what they like and don't like about their processes.

Mind mapping

Constructing mind maps can be a great technique to show a collection of ideas visually or develop an understanding that can be expanded on in front of other stakeholders. If you are new to a subject area, then you can visually show what areas you understand and allow other stakeholders to fill in the gaps for you. It can also be used for brainstorming different scenarios for a topic, planning out different tasks or helping to organize thoughts or brainstorm ideas with others.

For your mind map, start off with a central subject area drawn in the middle and branch outwards and at different angles to show related topics each time. One or two words should be sufficient, not complete sentences. The idea is to mimic thought patterns. Pictures can also be used in place of or alongside text. Mind maps can be used to aid meetings, as they are quick to produce and can incorporate ideas from others.

Mind maps can be used as a technique at any point during a change. I've included mind mapping as an elicitation technique, as it is not an end deliverable but more of a discovery tool to build up an understanding before using it as an input for something else.

CASE STUDY

See Figure 5.2 for a mind map appropriate to the Dream Phones case study. Sometimes a mind map is known as a brainstorming diagram or a rich picture if you are more creative with using diagrams rather than text.

You should be able to see from Figure 5.2 that using the subject area 'To part exchange old stock for new' helped to generate several ideas of what was required and further options from each idea.

FIGURE 5.2 Mind map

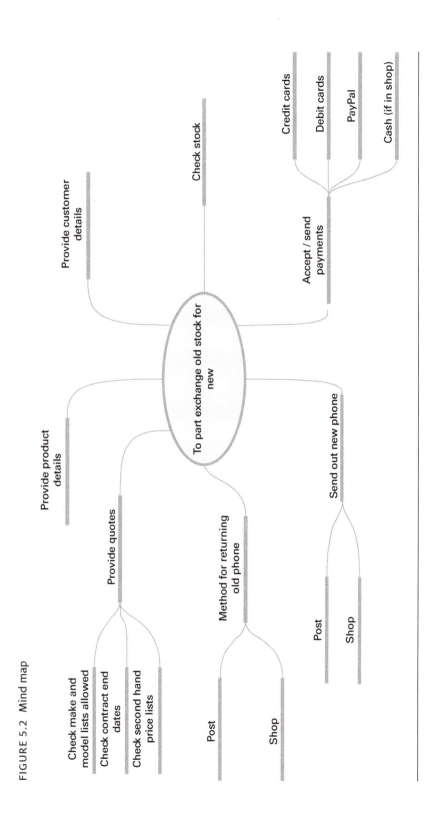

Business domain model

As well as eliciting business requirements by scrutinizing business processes, you can source them from the types of data required using business language. The business domain model is one of the best techniques for understanding types of data. This is because it identifies not just the data needed but how data can be grouped together and how they relate to each other. This model is useful for understanding business technical jargon and agreeing the same business terminology. This then avoids different language being used to mean the same thing and allows agreement on the same vocabulary and terms to avoid confusion. This technique is also useful for any changes that have any data associated with them. This applies where data need to be collected, changed, held, retrieved or communicated.

A business domain model starts off with subject areas being identified, together with the relationships between them. This is where it will contain high-level categories of data without going down into the detail of the attributes. Once the subject areas are identified the attributes can be added to the subject areas to represent the data required. A business domain model looks like an entity relationship diagram. An entity relationship diagram is associated with representing how the data should be built in the design stage. This includes design elements such as what data are needed to uniquely identify a record and how to join the entities together using common data attributes. As we just want to understand the business's data requirements and business concepts, the business domain model is appropriate, and the additional details associated with an entity relationship diagram are not required.

Entities   Subject areas are called entities and represented by placing the headings in a rectangular box, as shown in Figure 5.3, which includes examples of the types of data discovered using this approach.

FIGURE 5.3 Types of data

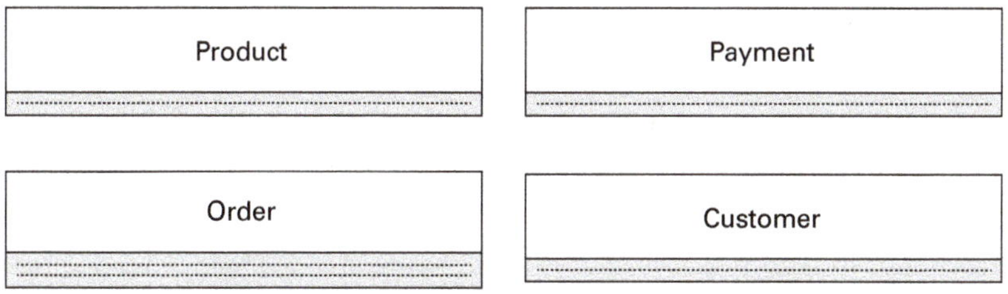

One of the good things this does is to get the stakeholders to tell you which words mean the same thing. You can get everyone to agree to use the same term. This can be reflected in the documentation and ensures consistency. I've managed to uncover as many as 10 different words my stakeholders were using in a meeting that all meant the same thing. They were all using these words interchangeably, and it wasn't until I did this exercise with them by writing each word on a flip chart that they realized how confusing it was for me. It was useful, because we were then able to agree one term and it made it much easier to understand the stakeholders' requirements.

ADDING ATTRIBUTES TO ENTITIES

An attribute is a characteristic of an entity. 'Product', shown in Figure 5.3, may have attributes such as product name, model or version. Attributes of a customer could be customer name, date of birth and National Insurance number. Attributes always belong to an entity. We do not need to be concerned about what attributes would be needed to join the entities together or worry about creating unique keys as part of business requirements elicitation.

ADDING RELATIONSHIPS BETWEEN ENTITIES

The reason why this technique is better than just listing the types of data your stakeholders are interested in is that it also helps you to explore the relationships between the data. The relationships describe how each entity is associated with another. Relationships are given names to describe how entities relate to one another, and the names are shown on a line drawn between the two entities that have an association. They can be given names in both directions, and the names are represented as verbs.

Relationships also have properties known as 'cardinality', and these are represented by symbols. Cardinality defines how many occurrences of a piece of data from one entity are defined compared to the entity it is related to. Examples of the different types of cardinality and corresponding symbols are shown in Figure 5.4. These cardinality symbols can be used to show the relationship properties between two entities.

If the relationship doesn't always happen, the 'one to one' or 'one to many' can be replaced with 'zero to one' or 'zero to many'. You only need a relationship to be shown once to an entity. As long as you can link the entities by going through other entities you do not have to ensure direct links to cater for every scenario.

FIGURE 5.4 Cardinality symbols

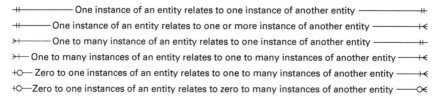

If there are any one to one relationships identified then you can combine them into one entity. This is where you start to establish attributes belonging to an entity. By the end of this approach you should end up with an understanding of what data are required to meet the business requirement and can relate this back to the objectives and goals identified. See the case study below, which provides an example of how this is done.

Understanding whether each piece of information has a one to one relationship or a one to many provides a greater insight into the data. It can also uncover missing requirements. The case study below provides examples of how this happens.

CASE STUDY

One of the objectives highlighted in Chapter 3 for our fictional mobile phone company Dream Phones was to understand what customers are ordering. When eliciting business requirements one approach could be to use a business domain model to understand the data required.

In a workshop with your stakeholders you would ask them to specify the types of data they need to know about from customers. You would write out the high-level headings represented in Figure 5.5 by product, order, customer and payment. Next you would ask about the relationships between them.

Using Figure 5.5 as an example, the following relationships have been identified:

- A customer places one or more orders.
- An order will be placed by one customer.
- An order includes one or more products.
- A product will be included in zero or more orders.
- An order requires zero or more payments.
- A payment is required by an order.

FIGURE 5.5 Business domain model

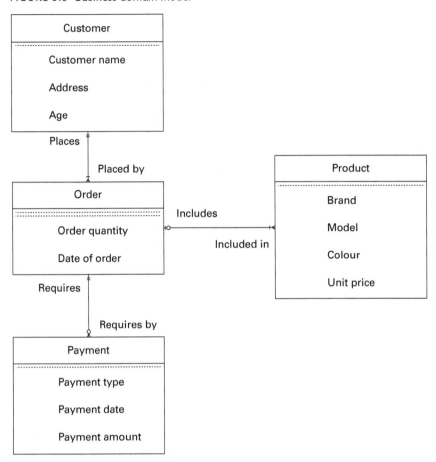

An example of how this also highlights what is required from the business requirements is that the relationships identified show that a customer can place an order without making a payment. This needs to be agreed with the business when defining the business requirements. It also shows that there is only one address allowed per customer. There may be a requirement to specify multiple addresses.

Attributes identified for a customer are customer name, address and age. When reviewing against the objective of understanding what customers are ordering you may want to challenge whether the company needs any other information related to customers. The goal behind this objective from looking at the goals and objectives set out in Chapter 3 was to predict market trends. Therefore, there may be a desire to understand cohorts of customers. A cohort is a set of characteristics that the customers may share, such as region, age or gender.

EXAMPLE

Business domain models provide a different perspective of asking about the requirements so may also uncover requirements that would have been missed otherwise. For example, I had documented the business processes of one business and identified the requirements from it. I then used this approach of asking the business to explain to me the types of data it used, what they were for and how they were updated. The business processes had shown that the data were updated by a third party only. However, when I questioned the business on all of the different types of data it emerged that the business itself needed a method for updating the data to provide information that it wasn't possible for the third party to provide. If this hadn't been realized it could have led to solutions not meeting the business requirements.

Business use case model

Business use case models identify all the user end goals for the project (known as use cases), all the stakeholders (known as human actors) involved and any systems (known as system actors) impacted.

A business use case model is an extended version of the context diagram covered in Chapter 3. The main difference is that the context diagram treats the project as a black box, which means it excludes what the project needs to do, whereas the business use case model is a white box approach and therefore includes the things required from the project. This helps towards understanding the areas of study for the project, who has an interest in it and the system interfaces. It is useful from an elicitation point of view because it is easy to draw out during workshops and enables each use case to be estimated and planned. A line is drawn between each actor and use case. Each use case can be estimated based on a size of small, medium and large and a complexity of simple, medium and complex. The number of workshops can be planned on this basis, along with which human actors to involve. This is especially useful if you are following an iterative approach, because breaking a project down into use cases enables you to do this. A use case is an end goal, so each one will deliver something in its entirety. It is also a powerful technique for enabling stakeholders to understand if the scope of the project is too big.

CASE STUDY

From a business perspective at project level, the business use case model in Figure 5.6 demonstrates the type of user end goals required for the fictional company Dream Phones. It shows at a high level the types of things that the business wants to achieve. These are represented by the ovals and are called use cases. The stick people are used to represent each of the stakeholders and are called actors. Figure 5.6 shows that marketing wants to be able to monitor trends and send marketing messages. Operations wants to be able to check stock, recycle old phones and send new phones. The customer wants to be able to order a new phone and recycle the old phone. The boundary box, if displayed around the use cases, is used to represent what will be included in the project to make the changes required.

FIGURE 5.6 Business use case model diagram

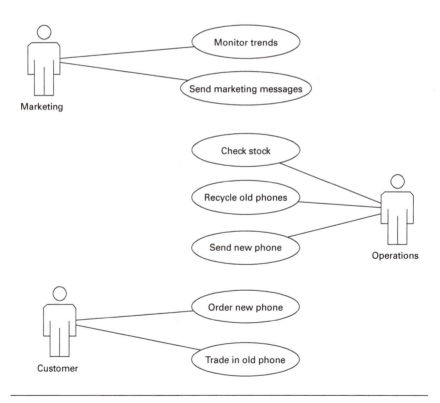

EXAMPLE

I was on a project where the business had written its own requirements and I had been asked to come on board at a later stage to provide traceability. The business requirements document was nearly 100 pages. It turned out that providing the solution had been overlooked owing to the complexity of the document. I went through the document, pulled out the use cases and translated them into a business use case model. There were 80 use cases. I was able to persuade the business to narrow down its scope, as viewing so many use cases in a diagram enabled the business to realize its expectation of all of it being delivered within a year was too high.

How do you formulate a good requirement?

There are several considerations to keep in mind when formulating a good requirement. This section provides a checklist for you to use.

Diagrams to group requirements

Resist the temptation to start writing out reams of requirements in full sentences. Using diagrams will be faster for gaining confirmation and avoiding ambiguity. Business requirements can be written once the diagrams are confirmed. Diagrams that can be used include business process modelling, mind maps and use case models, many of which are described in this book. It is important to group the requirements. Business processes identified can be used for grouping or by use case. It is important to take a top-down approach. The processes or the use cases in the business use case model help define the breadth of the scope. Drilling down into the detail by writing out the business requirements helps to ensure the breadth of the scope is not missed. It is then easier to see if requirements are being missed against a grouping.

Checking requirements are complete

Write out requirements and check they are complete, which means they must not leave anything outstanding. An example of a bad requirement that is not complete is one that states 'To be confirmed'. The whole point of obtaining sign-off on a document is to baseline the requirements that have been completed. You shouldn't be asking for approval if there are items outstanding in the requirements.

Checking requirements are non-ambiguous and verifiable

Requirements should be written out in such a way as to ensure they all can be understood and to avoid ambiguity. It is important to check that assumptions haven't been made. Just because it is obvious to the person who wrote the requirement what is meant doesn't mean it will be obvious to someone else reading the requirement. The requirements you write must be comprehensible even to new people joining the project, as you cannot always guarantee that the stakeholders will not change. People may leave halfway through a project, or new roles may be introduced later. At whatever stage people join the project they must be able to understand the requirements without huge amounts of interpretation. Ambiguity was also covered in Chapter 2, which explained how to recognize ambiguity when interacting with stakeholders and why it happened.

Words to be wary of in requirements include the following:

large;	user friendly;
many;	quickly;
small;	enhance;
appropriate;	minimize;
efficient;	maximize;
effective;	sufficient;
reliable;	adequate;
compatible;	support;
normal;	but not limited to.

This is because they may mean different things to different people. For example, I was in a meeting where everyone agreed that a large number of something was required. I asked each person around the table to say what number 'large' meant to them. The answers varied from 10 to millions. If I had not asked to verify what was meant, then the stakeholders could have left the room with completely different ideas in their heads of what 'large' meant.

When you write requirements, tie them to something measurable. This will also make them easier to verify and test. User acceptance testing is often based on what the business requirements specifies. Testers will not easily be able to write their test scripts unless you give them something to measure success with. If your requirement specifies that something must be adequate, how would they know what counted as a success?

CASE STUDY

Let's take the following business requirement provided earlier in the Dream Phones case study: 'To quote to the customer how much the second-hand mobile phones are worth based on the information received from the customer.'

This requirement could be improved by adding some success criteria to it or having a supplementary non-functional requirement. Non-functional requirements relate to the quality of the product. This could be adding how quickly the quote needs to be provided to the customer. This is important, because it will help influence the type of solutions that can be considered. 'To quote to the customer within one working day how much the second-hand mobile phones are worth based on the information received from the customer.'

Ensuring requirements are clear and concise

A good requirement must be clear and concise and not contain too much information. Details not specifically related to a requirement can be added as an appendix to the business requirements document.

It can be tempting to show off your business knowledge, but there is then the risk of overloading the readers with too much information and this could then water down what is meant by the requirement. Another related drawback is that the thicker the business requirements document is the harder it will be to get your stakeholders to review it. It will also make it more difficult to recognize duplications or missing requirements. This latter point can particularly be a problem if the requirements are collected from different stakeholders at different times. If different terminology has been used it might not even be easy to tell that the requirements overlap. Therefore, the clearer and more concise you can be, coupled with the earlier tip on grouping the requirements, the easier it will be to remove duplication.

As a guide, ensure you reference each of your requirements and that each requirement is no more than 30–50 words in length. Referencing your requirements will make it easier to talk about the different requirements listed and to obtain feedback for improvement. It is easier to give a reference number than to have to write out the whole requirement being discussed.

Any acronyms should be written out the first time they are used. Alternatively ensure they are explained in a glossary.

Ensuring requirements are consistent

This means ensuring consistent terminology throughout all the requirements you have elicited. Consistency will also help ensure your requirements are not duplicated. It is beneficial to be consistent with the terms used, because it makes it more obvious if any requirements have been repeated. The other problem that could occur is that requirements conflict with each other. If this happens then you may need to get the stakeholders concerned together to obtain a consensus.

Checking requirements are valuable

Each requirement provided comes at a cost. It is important that an investigation is conducted to check that the requirement is needed and that it is achievable given the dependencies and constraints.

When eliciting requirements ascertain at the same time the priority of the requirement, its rationale, the consequences if it is not delivered and how it relates back to the objectives and problem statement. Just because a requirement is elicited doesn't necessarily mean it should end up in the requirements document. Each one should be challenged to check it is achieving the aim of the project and contributing to the project's success. Allowing unnecessary requirements will add to the cost and the risk of not completing the project successfully.

Ensuring requirements are feasible

Feasibility is important. If there are dependencies, then the requirement may not be feasible. Dependencies may rely on other projects to put something in place first. If this is outside the control of your project, then further investigation is required as to how big an impact this will have. If it looks unlikely the dependency will be removed in time, then it may be the case that you document the requirement in the appendix as a future requirement for another phase. This way it doesn't lose visibility and so the requirement can be considered again in the future. It also helps the stakeholders understand their requirement hasn't been forgotten and enables a conversation as to why it is not for the current phase.

Another reason for a lack of feasibility may be related to constraints. Constraints may be related to budget, timescales, resources and capability, for example. It may not be possible to know with absolute certainty about these at this stage of the project, but if there are any indicators then this must be taken into consideration. Getting early involvement from solution subject matter experts will help in understanding these. If possible, get them added as a sign-off so they have a vested interest in understanding the document and can then help ensure they feed back any potential feasibility issues. The sooner these are understood the more likely it is to overcome them if the requirement is integral to the success of the project.

Ensuring requirements are non-solution-specific

The business requirements documented in the business requirements document should not be solution-specific. The document should not specify the method for doing something but should just contain what needs to be addressed. If you take the examples I provided earlier, you will notice that none of them contain a solution:

- To enable customers to provide their old phone details. Details to include are make, model number, condition, original provider of the phone and contract end date.
- To quote to customers how much the second-hand mobile phones are worth based on the information received from the customer.
- To enable customers to return their old mobile phones.
- To enable customers to provide details of the new phone they require. Details are make, model number, colour and capacity.
- To enable customers to provide customer and payment details.
- To receive the old mobile phones and provide the new ones requested.
- To recycle old mobile phones received.

The solution may have been specified by the stakeholder. For example, to enable customers to provide their old phone details, one suggestion could be to send emails out directing customers to provide their details. It is important however to remove such suggestions, as they are solutions that could change. Later, the solution that makes most sense might be to create an online form, which was not considered at the time the requirements were written. You may have to ask why or enquire what stakeholders get from something several times to get to the business requirement.

What goes into a business requirements document?

The purpose of the business requirements document is to set out the business's requirements to achieve the scope, goals, objectives and problems identified for change. As outlined above in relation to formulating the requirements, this document should be non-solution-specific. There is normally more than one solution to a business requirement, and business requirements are likely to be more static than solution requirements. The document therefore provides the foundations for understanding the solution requirements as part of the design phase. An example template is provided in Chapter 9.

The benefit of documenting the business requirements is that it ensures all your stakeholders are thinking the same thing. When ideas are in people's heads there is no certainty of consensus until they are written down. The previous section provided tips on how to write the business requirements so they are easy to read and understand. Another benefit is the prioritization of business requirements. This will make it easier to judge what solutions are more suitable and what can be dropped if time or cost doesn't allow.

A typical structure of the traditional business requirements document is shown in the following subsections.

Header title page

This is the front cover. It contains the name of the change/project name, version number, author and file of where it is stored. Before it is signed off it must be clearly labelled with a draft watermark and must start with a version of 0.1. If it is distributed and then changes are made the version number must be updated to 0.2. This will then go up by 0.1 each subsequent time it is changed and distributed. Only when it is signed off will it change to version 1 and the draft watermark be removed. Versioning is important to ensure each stakeholder is reading the correct version of the document and for traceability.

Contents

The contents can be autogenerated in Word if you make use of the heading functionality.

Document control

There should be a record of all the versions, updated each time a new version is created, showing what changes were made each time. This is also known as version control.

A list of the signatories is needed. It is important to ensure there is a representative for each business area impacted. You do not need to repeat the signatories as reviewers if they are listed here. Think about how many signatories you have and whether the number is appropriate. If there are more than necessary, the sign-off period will be greater than it needs to be, because it always takes time and effort chasing sign-offs. You should not have more than one sign-off per business area identified as a rule.

A list or reviewers should be provided, including name, role in the change and job title. It is useful to record the latest version of the business requirements document the reviewers have seen.

You may want to include a separate table for acknowledgements if stakeholders have contributed but are not reviewers or signatories. This helps identify all the people who have contributed.

Include a role in the reviewer section for peer review. Before the other stakeholders get sent any version of the document, ask the peer reviewer to review the document first as part of best practice. This should be someone who ideally is not involved with the project. This person will then be able to check more easily that anyone new to the project could pick up the document and understand it. It is very easy when people are heavily involved in a change for them to build assumptions in without realizing it.

Glossary

I would recommend having the glossary near the beginning of the document so that people can become familiar with the terminology and understand any abbreviations used before they read the rest of the document.

Executive summary

This is a summary of the change for those who have limited time to understand the document and just need to understand the essence of the change.

It also helps to set the context before providing any of the detail. Consequently, it should not be any more than one or two pages.

It should contain the following:

- Introduction: information needed to understand the need for change, which should be no more than half a page.

- Project objectives: the objectives agreed as part of the project.

- Associated documentation: any material or previous documents relating to the change can be listed here.

- Items in scope: a list of items within the scope of the project. This may be taken from the items identified as part of the scoping (see Chapter 3).

- Items out of scope: a list of items out of the scope of the project. This may be taken from the items identified as not part of the scoping (see Chapter 3).

Business processes

Ideally the business processes are defined prior to the writing of the business requirements document and signed off beforehand. If this hasn't been possible, they should be included here. They will help you to understand the requirements, because each process identified may have requirements behind it, and this will help you to group the requirements as discussed earlier in this chapter. See Chapter 4 for more detail on defining the end to end business processes. Make sure you include a key to explain to the reader what the symbols mean. Alternatively this could be added to the appendix.

Business use case model

Once the business processes have been defined, a conversation can be had on which parts of the process should be in scope. This will help you to build your business use case model. See earlier in the chapter for an explanation of how to put one together.

Business requirements

The business requirements are often set out in narrative format, breaking down all the different types of needs the business has in order to meet the change objectives, solve its problems and be successful. Each requirement should have a reference, group it belongs to, narrative description, priority, source and rationale for being included.

References are required to make it easy to navigate when obtaining feedback. These should then not change, to ensure traceability. A common mistake is to renumber the references when additional requirements are added. Please don't do this, as it will just cause confusion as to when to use the old or the new references. It is more important to keep the original references even if they then aren't listed in numerical order.

Prioritizing requirement guidelines will be covered in more detail in Chapter 7. To briefly summarize, a rating should be given as to how important each requirement is. This is needed because each requirement will come at a cost. Change must be delivered within constraints such as budget and time. If a requirement has a high cost associated with it and is desirable rather than essential then it easier to make a judgement on whether it should be delivered compared to delivering other requirements that are of higher value. Estimation of how much it will cost to deliver the change will need to be undertaken after the business requirements document is signed off. If it is more than budgeted or will take longer to deliver than required, decisions need to be made. It will be easier to make decisions on what should be delivered if priority of the requirements is understood.

A source should be added to name the person who has specified the requirement. This is needed so that it is understood who to go back to if there are any additional queries about the requirement.

A rationale should be given individually for each requirement. This is to provide the reasons why each requirement is needed. The rationale must be tailored and not generic. This can be difficult if the change relates to a regulatory project. However, regulatory wording can have various interpretations that the business might want to adopt and take forward. In addition, requirements may have different timescales. Only day 1 requirements would have the highest priority, and their rationales can be given here.

Logs

Logs should list all of the assumptions, issues, risks, decisions and dependencies that have been identified whilst documenting the requirements. They should be sent to the project manager and added to the central project risks, assumptions, issues and dependencies (RAID) log. More detail is provided about assumptions, dependencies, risks and issues in the remainder of this chapter.

Appendices

Create appendices for any details that do not fit within the main body of the document. If there are examples of forms or reports then these could be added here. If requirements have been de-scoped, you could create an appendix for them, which could include the reasons why they were discounted. This will help prevent stakeholders inadvertently reopening the debate. It will also give the comfort factor that these requirements are recorded somewhere if required for a future project or phase.

What are assumptions, dependencies, risks and issues?

This section sets out the differences between assumptions, dependencies, risks and issues. These factors need to be added to a project's central log (the RAID log), where risks, assumptions, issues and dependencies can be tracked. They are normally managed by the project manager. However, as part of working in a team you will be expected to look out for risks and mention them. They will often be found as part of the business requirements document, because they will come up as part of the requirements elicitation and documentation process. It is therefore best to capture them when they happen, particularly if they are going to have an impact on the business requirements. I set out a description for each below, because it is important to categorize each one correctly.

Assumptions

An assumption is something that hasn't been confirmed but a belief to help enable the project to make decisions and estimates. If the assumptions are later found to be incorrect they could have a significant impact on the project.

Assumptions can be based on business strategy, project methodologies, technology or design considerations, facilities or infrastructure, among others. The more assumptions that can be validated up front the more confidence that can be had in the estimates.

Dependencies

A dependency exists when the change in scope is reliant on something else happening outside of the scope of the requirements being documented.

A dependency could exist because of reliance on another project to deliver an output first or because of a decision that needs to be made or an action required by someone else.

Risks

A risk is something that hasn't happened yet but is a concern. If it did happen it would cause a delay or disrupt the project in some way. Examples include:

- availability of stakeholders' time;
- failure to identify all the stakeholders who need to specify the requirements for the proposed change;
- decisions not being made in a timely manner to progress the requirements within the planned timescales;
- stakeholders being identified incorrectly or at the wrong level;
- requirements being identified that are not feasible given the constraints.

It is common for business analysts to come across risks before anyone else. This is because they are engaged with several stakeholders at one time, have a strong understanding of the project, are often involved with a project the whole way through and provide traceability. If there are any warning signs, then they are normally in the best position to spot them. It is therefore important that the business analyst feels confident about how to raise awareness of risks and understands the risk management process.

Think about the likelihood and impact if it happened when considering a risk. This will help the project manager understand what action is needed and how urgently to take it. To mitigate a risk the project manager may choose to accept it, transfer it elsewhere or do something to remove or reduce it. Ratings for likelihood and impact tend to be categorized as high, medium or low or given a score rating. It is important to get these ratings correct, as the project manager may not want to accept a risk if the likelihood and impact are high.

It is good practice to review the risks on the RAID log regularly to check you haven't seen any indicators that change the status of the likelihood and impact. A risk becomes an issue when it has happened, so it is beneficial to mitigate the risks to prevent them turning into issues. You may also have some options to help the project manager to identify the mitigating actions that can be used against a risk.

Reviewing risks is a good way of ensuring any concerns or worries you may have are recognized, and it is a good communication tool.

Issues

An issue is something that has happened and is causing a delay or disrupting the project in some way. Risks may turn into issues if they turn into reality. Decisions need to be made and problems solved to remove issues.

What are the implications of mixing up business requirements, assumptions, dependencies, risks and issues?

Business requirements establish things that need to happen for the business to achieve its objectives. They are turned into solution requirements, and then there is development, software purchased, configuration or outsourcing to enable the business requirements to be fulfilled. If business requirements are specified as assumptions, then this implies the changes required have already been satisfied and nothing will happen to them. If business requirements are specified as dependencies, then this implies that the changes must be carried out before the solution can be delivered and that they are out of scope for the delivery of the business requirements in the business requirements document. If business requirements are specified as risks, or things that are in danger of not happening, this then becomes likely, because they then aren't down as requirements to be delivered. If business requirements are specified as issues, then they are identified as already a problem even though they are things the business wants to happen as part of the change.

If assumptions are specified as requirements then something could get delivered that is already fulfilled and not required. If risks or issues are specified as requirements then this could cause confusion as to what is required and could hold up progress. If a dependency is specified as a requirement then you could end up with duplication of effort.

06

System context/understanding requirements

Introduction

The hierarchy of requirements was outlined in Chapter 5 as a basis for understanding requirements. To recap, requirements are first defined at a high level to understand the problem and objectives. They are then related to what the business wants in order to meet the objectives. Finally, a lower level of detail is established. This lower level of detail helps to inform the business analysis about the functionality of the system needed to solve the problems or complete the objectives. This chapter will focus on the techniques you can use to analyse or document the system requirements. These can also be referred to as solution requirements to reflect the fact that not all solutions will be based on an IT system.

Systems or solutions can be big and complicated, so techniques have been created to ensure that the breadth and depth of information required is obtained. They are based on tried and tested industry standards that can be replicated to ensure the best results. Solution requirements can be functional or non-functional. There are methods that can be used to uncover and document these differences.

Often companies will look to third parties to provide the solutions, so I also cover considerations and approaches for this context. This means providing the requirements for the procurement process to choose the best third party supplier for the organization's needs. By the end of this chapter you will understand what involvement you might have in this situation and how you can add value.

When working with agile projects, there are several recognized frameworks that set out different approaches that can be used. These are also summarized to provide guidance on what each approach sets out to achieve.

Questions answered in this chapter for understanding system requirements

- What are the techniques for understanding and documenting functional requirements (use case models, use cases, user stories, storyboarding and traditional table format)?
- How do you deal with global non-functional requirements?
- How do you adapt requirements for commercial off the shelf packages?
- What is involved in the procurement process and how can business analysis help?
- How do you evaluate responses from software providers?
- What are the approaches for agile projects?

What are the techniques for understanding and documenting functional requirements (use case models, use cases, user stories, storyboarding and traditional table format)?

In this section, five techniques will be detailed to help with understanding and documenting functional requirements: use case models, use cases, user stories, storyboarding and the traditional table format. These techniques are invaluable for business analysts, and each fits with different approaches and circumstances. One or more of these can be used at a time, so it is useful to be familiar with each of them. The more types of techniques you understand and can apply, the more equipped you will be to get the requirements right and not miss anything out. It would be impossible to be a subject matter expert for every business area, so the questions and techniques provided in this book will equip you to be able to gather the requirements with little or no previous business knowledge.

Use case models

WHAT IS A USE CASE MODEL?
A use case model can be constructed to categorize the work to be done and the human and/or system interfaces that impact it. Chapter 5 covered the use case model at business level. Here the use case model will be explained at the solutions/systems level.

REASONS FOR USING THE USE CASE MODEL TECHNIQUE

This is such a useful technique because it summarizes what is in scope on one page in an accessible diagram. Use case models have huge benefits to a wide range of stakeholders. For example, they are an effective method for breaking down the changes required into manageable chunks. This is particularly useful for large projects and for planning the work required. It can then help with delivering the changes iteratively, and it can also be used in a waterfall or an agile approach. See Figure 6.1 for an example of a use case model structure.

PUTTING TOGETHER A USE CASE MODEL

When putting together a use case model the first step is to identify the actors who will need to interact with the solution. An actor can be human related or system related.

- Human actors can be outside the organization, for example the suppliers, regulators or customers. They can also be related to a department, team or role.

- System actors are those systems that are not part of the solution being changed but need to interact with it in some way, for example by sending data to it or being a recipient of data.

Actors are represented in a use case model using stick figures. They are then labelled underneath with their name. System-related actors have the word 'system' in capital letters after their label. Actors should only be included if they interact directly with the system and have specific goals for using it. Each actor is given a unique reference, starting with ACT001, which increases by one each time.

FIGURE 6.1 Blank use case model

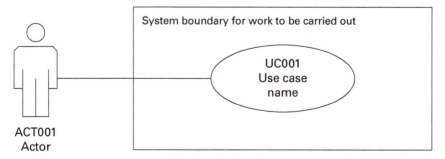

System boundaries are represented using rectangular boxes to show the system changes scoped for the project. The system boundary should be labelled with the type of system being represented. Examples of system boundaries are administration systems, customer portals, intranets, company internets and customer relationship management systems.

Use cases are represented by oval shapes, which look like squashed circles or rugby balls. Users who aren't familiar with use case terminology could use the word 'goals' instead. The goal of each of the actors identified earlier is summarized in a few words in terms of interacting with the system. The structure always starts with a verb, which is followed by a noun.

The use case is written from the point of view of actors and describes what they want to do with the system. It can be difficult to pitch this at the right level without breaking it down to too low a level. It is meant to fit on one page and be easy to read, as the use case model is a foundation for more detailed requirements. There are several methods for identifying a use case at the right level for a system use case model:

1 Identify the inputs to and outputs from the system for each of the actors. This is useful information for further analysis and will help answer the question of what the goal is for each input and output.

2 If there have previously been process modelling diagrams put together you may be able to identify the use cases by agreeing which processes will need to interact with the system.

3 A use case will need to have a number of lower-level interactions between it and the actors concerned to achieve the goal, and a number of different scenarios to achieve it, with 7- to 12-step interactions ideal. If there are only a few steps the use case is too low-level. More than 12 steps and the use case is probably too big.

Each use case is labelled with a unique reference in a similar way to the actors. Each unique label starts with UC001 and increases sequentially by one each time. This becomes the use case's unique reference and shouldn't be changed once assigned. Unlike business processes, use cases do not have to be kept in a particular order.

Lines are then drawn to show which use cases relate to each of the actors. At systems level there is normally just one actor associated with each use case. If there are more than one, then it means that an actor is interacting with the system for the same purpose. This may mean that the roles are the same and can be taken on by one actor. Or it could mean that the use case has slightly different goals between the two actors and needs to be split out.

There are two other types of use cases that you might want to consider. These are called the 'includes use case' and the 'extends use case'. They aren't always necessary, but help to break out the work further if required.

Includes use cases are use cases containing several steps that can be used by other use cases. Rather than repeating the same steps each time, the steps can be separated into their own use case. An arrow is then drawn to it from the main use case. The syntax is an arrow and two chevrons either side of the narrative word 'include', shown as <<include>>. It is called an includes use case when those steps must happen for another use case to be achieved.

Extends use cases are optional steps that can be taken from another use case. The syntax is an arrow in the opposite direction to that for the includes use case and has the narrative word 'extend' with two chevrons either side, shown as <<extend>>. The arrow goes from the goal containing the optional steps to the related use case.

CASE STUDY

Now let's apply this knowledge to the Dream Phones case study. See Figure 6.2 for an example of a use case model for creating a website to allow customers to buy phones online.

The main actor is the customer. The goals a customer could have are to browse phones, search phones, conduct phone finder questionnaire, compare new phones, view product information, choose a product package, add extras and buy new phone. The goals have been obtained by conducting customer research and competitor analysis. They are represented by the oval shapes and are called use cases. They are enclosed in a boundary rectangular box that represents the company internet. The use cases in it are what the system must be able to do. 'Add extras' and 'Buy new phone' are extend use cases of 'Choose product package'. This is because the customer has to be able to choose the product package before being able to add extras or buy the phone, but it isn't compulsory. Customers may change their minds or just be looking at options.

FIGURE 6.2 Use case model diagram at systems level

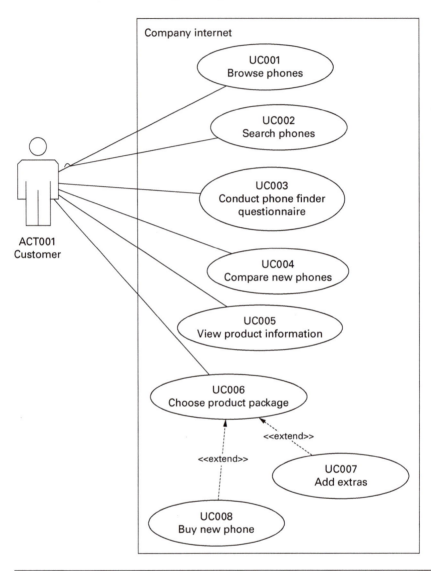

Use cases

WHAT IS A USE CASE?

A use case breaks down the work into smaller chunks by identifying user end goals from the perspective of the interactions between users and external systems. It sets out all the different scenarios and interactions that can occur using the concept of a happy path followed by any alternatives or exceptions that could happen.

REASONS FOR USING USE CASES

Use cases are very structured, and help ensure requirements are not repeated, irrelevant, inconsistent or ambiguous, as can happen with traditional wordier methods. It is best to use this method on large projects with new features and functionality where system development is to be written from scratch. It may feel over-engineered if used on small changes. Regardless of what technique you are using, the standard headings used in this method provide a list of valuable questions that can be used to elicit the solution requirements whether you end up documenting them in this way or not.

PUTTING TOGETHER A USE CASE

There are two approaches: the casual approach and the formal approach. In the next case study, I have demonstrated the differences by illustrating both approaches. The casual approach is the one I would recommend if timescales are really tight and you need to get a first draft out quickly or if you are just using it as an elicitation technique. Developers who are writing code from scratch tend to prefer the formal approach, because it tells them what is required from the system at a low level by detailing the interactions between each actor identified and the system. It covers the main flow they need to code and any exceptions and alternatives. This is one of the most comprehensive methods for documenting system functional requirements.

Use cases are technology-neutral and do not tend to detail global non-functional requirements (NFRs). The technologies fall under the remit of the solution architect. The global non-functional requirements are covered later in this chapter.

A use case is typically written in a table format. One of these is populated for each use case identified in the use case model. The headings below cover each of the areas that are required and some guidelines for populating them.

Use case name: This can be taken from the use case model. The use case name starts with a reference beginning with UC and a unique reference number starting with 001. Each additional use case goes up in sequence by one each time. A very brief description follows in a couple of words, which is always an action word followed by a noun.

Use case description: This enables a fuller description to be given of the use case in a sentence. It starts with the narrative: 'This use case occurs when...'.

Priority: An understanding can be specified here on the importance of the use case. Would the system be worth developing without it? A priority level of high should only be given to those that fall into this category. A priority level of medium should be given to those that are still needed but could be part of a second phase if time or budget don't allow them in the first phase. A priority level of low can be given to those use cases that are nice to have.

Justification: This is to explain why the use case is needed and to supplement the priority given.

Pre-conditions: These identify the state of the system before the use case.

Post-conditions: These identify the state of the system after the use case.

Main flow: In the formal approach this details the main scenario that occurs in sequence order. It typically starts with describing how the actor starts to use the system. The starting line format should be:

- This use case starts when the <add actor name> chooses to <add use case name>

Each interaction back and forth should then be described between the actor and the system. Each sequence step is numbered.

When describing interactions, at the beginning of each sentence the description should start by showing whether the interaction is coming from the actor or the system. A verb should then be used to describe the action taking place. It's important to agree consistency with the wording used. Here are some examples of the type of wording to use:

The system reads	The system requests
The system displays	The system sends
The system lists	The system verifies
The system records	The actor chooses
The system updates	The actor confirms
The system deletes	

Always write each step from the point of view of the source, for example actor or system. Each step should be aimed at moving the scenario forward in the process. Therefore, do not include a description that relates to the interface but include one that relates to the achievements required for each step. As a guide, there should be between 7 and 12 steps in a main flow.

A tip for writing use cases is to describe all the data that need to be actioned in one step. Therefore, try to avoid the following:

1 The system requests name

2 The actor enters name

3 The system requests address

4 The actor enters address

A better way to approach this is the following:

1 The system requests customer details

2 The actor enters customer details

A different technique can then be used in conjunction with a use case to explain what the customer details consist of. This could be a business domain model (see below in this chapter). Another alternative could be:

1 The system requests name and address

2 The actor enters name and address

The format for ending a use case at the end of the sequence of steps should be:

- The use case ends

In the casual approach the main flow and alternative flow are merged together and just contain paragraphs giving a high-level description rather than sequence steps back and forth.

Alternative flow: This portion should contain all the alternative flows that can happen. Walk through each step identified in the main flow and determine whether any other steps can happen and in what circumstances. It may be that there are only some alternative steps, which may either then end or merge back into the main flow.

Alternative paths start with the narrative:

- The alternative flow occurs when

To signify when an alternative flow occurs the numbering convention should use the same number as the sequence step in the main flow to show it's an alternative to the main flow from that point. It should then be followed with the letter 'a' if it is the first alternative flow or 'b' for the second alternative flow and so on. Each sequence step should then be numbered. Refer to the next case study to see this in practice.

Sometimes there is a separate section created for exceptions to handle error messages and the types of scenarios where errors could occur. My preference is to record them as alternative flows.

Special requirements: This section contains any non-functional requirements specific to the use case or business rules to be adhered to. This isn't a mandatory section and is only populated when applicable.

CASE STUDY

Table 6.1 is an example of a formal use case for the fictional company Dream Phones. This is based on the use case UC003 – Conduct phone finder questionnaire.

Table 6.2 is an example of the casual version of the use case UC003 – Conduct phone finder questionnaire.

TABLE 6.1 Formal use case table structure

Use case name:	UC003 – Conduct phone finder questionnaire.
Use case description:	This use case occurs when the customer requests help with choosing a new phone.
Priority:	Medium.
Justification:	Customer research has shown that customers often want help choosing a new phone and it is part of their phone buying experience.
Pre-conditions:	None.
Post-conditions:	A phone package that matches the customer's choices has been displayed with an option to purchase it.
Main flow:	1. This use case starts when the ACT001 – Customer chooses to conduct the phone finder questionnaire process.
	2. The system displays usage details from a usage type list.
	3. The actor chooses one or more usage details.
	4. The system displays brands from a brand list.
	5. The actor chooses one or more brands.
	6. The system displays a choice of phone sizes.
	7. The actor chooses a phone size.
	8. The system calculates a budget based on the average package options price from the customer's answers.
	9. The actor changes or confirms the budget.
	10. The system displays the best matched package option and product details based on the answers in the phone finder questionnaire.
	11. The use case ends.

(continued)

TABLE 6.1 (*Continued*)

Alternative flow:	1a.	The alternative flow occurs when the actor has obtained the results from filling out the questionnaire previously.
	1a1.	Go to step 10 in main flow.
	10a.	The alternative flow occurs when the actor wishes to know the difference in package options if he/she lowers his/her budget.
	10a1.	The system displays the best matched package option and product details based on the next cheapest phone package.
	10a2.	Go to step 11 in main flow.
	10b.	The alternative flow occurs when the actor wishes to know the difference in package options if he/she raises his/her budget.
	10b1.	The system displays the best matched package option and product details based on the budget being the next most expensive phone package.
	10b2.	Go to step 11 in main flow.
Special requirements:		Only one best option should be displayed at any one time.

TABLE 6.2 Informal use case table structure

Use case name:	UC003 – Conduct phone finder questionnaire.
Use case description:	This use case occurs when the customer requests help with choosing a new phone.
Priority:	Medium.
Justification:	Customer research has shown that customers often want help choosing a new phone and it is part of their phone buying experience.
Pre-conditions:	None.
Post-conditions:	A phone package that matches the customer's choices has been displayed with an option to purchase it.
Main flow:	A customer wants to work out what phone package and phone would be best for him/her. The customer will need to be provided with questions on usage type, brand preferences, phone size preference and budget. The web page will need to ask the customer these questions and then provide him/her with a recommendation based on the answers. It will need to allow the customer to alter the budget and provide the customer with phone and package alternatives if he/she raises or lowers the budget. It should remember the previous results if the customer has previously filled out the questionnaire.

User stories

WHAT IS A USER STORY?

A user story focuses on understanding the user's need, the user's thought process and how the user will behave. The user stories do not provide the amount of detail provided by use cases or other more formal requirements documentation methods.

There is a big emphasis on collaboration and self-organizing teams with this technique. User stories are designed in such a way as to instigate conversations between the business, product owner and development teams. They are designed to capture a high-level description of a software feature from an end user perspective. They should be understandable to both business and technical stakeholders.

A user story is structured in the following type of format:

- As a <user role>
  I want to <action>
  So that <achieves following successful outcome>

A user role is any type of person who will interact with the solution. The person could be an external end user, internal user, employee or supplier, for example. An action is based on what action the user role wants to perform. A successful outcome states what the user role wants to achieve by being able to complete the stated action.

REASONS FOR USING USER STORIES

User stories typically feature in agile software development. Agile principles are based on providing software through continuous delivery and measuring the outcomes. Unlike the case in the waterfall approach there isn't a formal solution requirements document, and user stories do not need to be formally signed off, because it is the outcome of the software that is seen as more important.

With the software being delivered continuously there isn't a long wait to find out whether the requirements have been interpreted correctly. Changes are easily adopted, so if the software isn't right it can be recognized and dealt with accordingly.

There are no hard rules about having to create user stories in agile, but it is a popular method. This technique is in line with the agile methodology of having conversations and viewing outcomes in a relatively short period of time. The aim of user stories is to help shift the focus from writing to talking.

ACCEPTANCE CRITERIA

Every user story must have acceptance criteria. This is separate from the structuring of a user story in the 'As a <user role>, I want to <action>, so that <achieves following successful outcome>' style (described above). In agile more detail is added as and when it is needed. This is often called 'grooming the backlog' or 'refinement'. Acceptance criteria are added before work can start on the user story. This provides the detail that you would typically expect from a functional requirement setting out the functionality required for each of the different scenarios that need to be met and the business rules. This is to make sure there is a consensus, the developers know what to build and a judgement can be made as to when the user story has been completed. It will also help with checking that each scenario is tested successfully. Any non-functional requirements that are specific to a user story will also be added as acceptance criteria. More detail on global non-functional requirements can be found later in this chapter.

Acceptance criteria don't have to be in a specific format. However, one popular format method for acceptance criteria is called behaviour driven development (BDD). This sets out all the different scenarios that need to be met, which enables the testers to test all the scenarios to ensure the goal of the user story is complete. This format is also recognized as being useful for setting up automated testing. The format is:

- Given <a context> when <this event occurs> then <this happens>

USER STORY HIERARCHY

There is a hierarchy associated with user stories. Strategic high-level planning of releases and communication of the vision can be done using the high-level stories, whilst daily planning and doing the work will require the lower-level user stories. The reason for this hierarchy is to make it easier to put the user stories together using a top-down approach, to be able to communicate the right level of detail to different stakeholders and to make it easier to plan. The hierarchy from the highest level down is the following:

- Themes: A theme is a high-level subject heading, normally consisting of one or two words. This is at the highest level, where all of the stories underneath a theme can be grouped under this heading.

- Epics: An epic is a user story that is too big to be delivered in an iteration or sprint. An iteration or sprint is a short time period, normally two to four weeks, where parts of the solution can be delivered to show some outcomes for review.

- User stories: A user story is the level required to deliver within an iteration or sprint time period something that is of value to the business.

- Tasks: Tasks are added to user stories to indicate the work that needs to be carried out to deliver the user story. Tasks are added by all the different people in the team who need to do work on the user story. They are often tracked, and a user story cannot be completed until all the tasks identified are closed.

Writing user stories

User stories can be identified using a variety of different methods. They are then written up using the top-down hierarchy approach and refined continually over time according to the level of priority provided by the product owner. Priority is based on delivering the features and user stories that provide the greatest amount of value first. Refinement is normally a collaborative effort so is not down to one person to do on his or her own.

User stories are customer-centric, so it is important to make sure each user story is feasible and written from a technology and business perspective.

Each user story must be independent. This makes the user stories easier to prioritize and estimate. User stories form the basis for a conversation between the team members so should not be too prescriptive. When breaking down user stories it is important to make sure they are goal based and not part of a process. This is because each user story delivered must have value to the user. If the user story is just a step in a process to produce a goal, then it will not deliver value until all the steps towards the goal are achieved. User stories must be broken down until they are small enough to be delivered within a sprint time period. This may mean splitting down a user story several times until this criterion is met.

Splitting user stories out over iterations/sprints

There are guidelines that can be followed to help break down the user stories into smaller component parts that can then be refined later to enable development efforts to be realized sooner and to keep development iterative.

Figure 6.3 provides some ideas for how to split out user stories to get something delivered more quickly and provide the greatest amount of value. When this happens refined user stories will need to be added to enhance the functionality further with what was previously left out. It is important to be

FIGURE 6.3 Splitting user stories

Splitting user stories

- Plan these out separately
- Defer such as performance
- One path at a time
- Limit amount provided

- User roles/personas
- Non-functional requirements
- Scenarios
- Acceptance criteria
- Restrict between create, update, read and delete

- Business rules
- Operations allowed

- Defer business rules

- Sequence flow
- Platforms
- Data

- Focus on small number of steps
- Selection of technologies and browsers
- Data needed first and parameters

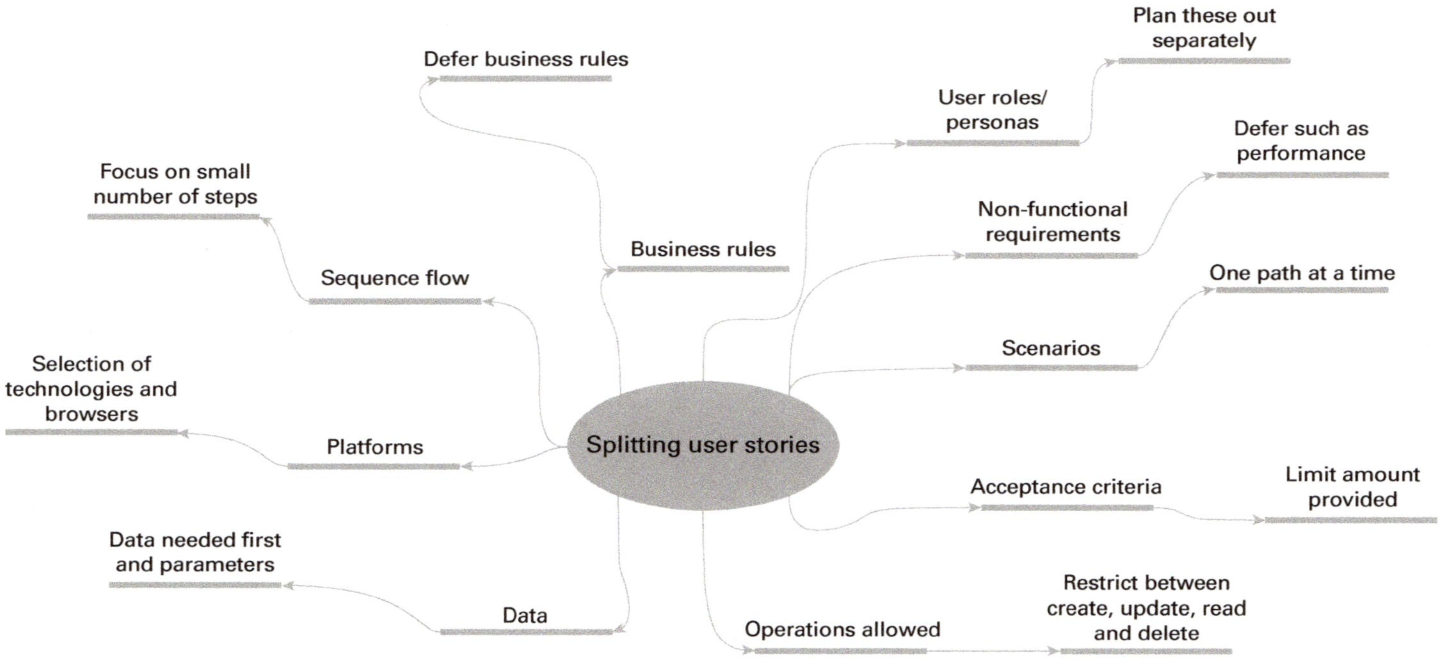

able to slice the user stories vertically, so they are delivering business value rather than just a step towards a goal. The amount of effort you will need to put in to divide the user stories will depend on the amount of effort estimated to deliver the user stories and how fast the team can work.

User stories ready for development criteria

Owing to the iterative nature of agile projects, user stories do not need to be fully formed until they are needed for the development stage. The continual learning and adaptation environments of projects might cause later user stories to change, so the requirements process is about having them ready at the right time. It is recommended you set out a definition of 'ready criteria' so it is clear when to hand the user stories over for development. This provides the team with what is required for a user story and gives them the opportunity to challenge if those items are not provided.

Here are some examples that fit with the definition of ready criteria:

- There is a consensus in the team that the story is ready.
- What is required from the point of view of users has been defined.
- The user story is independent of other stories and can be developed on its own without impacting others.
- The user story adds value to the product being developed for the customer or business.
- There are clear acceptance criteria setting out the scenarios that need to be met. The scenarios must include alternatives and exceptions in addition to the main flow.
- The user story has been classified as the next level of priority to be addressed in the product backlog. Work should focus its efforts in priority order based on business value.
- It should be possible to estimate the effort required of each user story.
- The definition of ready criteria helps developers and testers understand when the new functionality is ready to test and what scenarios need to be included.
- The user story must be feasible and have no dependencies preventing it from being carried forward.
- If working in sprints or iterations, then the user story must be broken down enough to develop in the time period. 'Sprints and iterations' are an

agile terminology used to signify the time chunks of work to be developed and tested. This will typically be two to four weeks. Companies new to agile might have this extended to six weeks. The time allowed for an iteration or sprint is agreed in advance.

- It must be clear how the user story will be demonstrated and played back.

User stories in Agile are place holders for conversations and are to be supplemented with additional information such as user journeys, screen mock ups and architectural designs. Therefore, they shouldn't be overly complicated or burdensome to produce. When handing over to developers it is useful to go through the user stories in conjunction with walking through the screen mock ups.

PRODUCT BACKLOG

User stories are often added to what is known in agile as the product backlog. Once they are added to the product backlog they are also referenced as product backlog items (PBIs). Additional supporting information such as screen mock ups, designs, acceptance criteria can then be attached to a user story in the product backlog.

CASE STUDY

An example of a user story for the fictional phone company Dream Phones could be:

- As a customer
  I want to conduct a phone finder questionnaire
  So that I can find out what phone package will meet my needs.

This would be classified as an epic, as the story is too big to deliver in an iteration or sprint.
  The story could be split into smaller user stories such as:

- As a customer I want to find out what phone packages are suitable based on my budget so that I can see what phone packages I can afford.

Storyboarding

WHAT IS A STORY BOARD?

Story boards act as a low-fidelity prototype to set out how the actual solution will work without the expense of building it first. This approach can include visual interfaces required of the solution and the user interactions between them. If there are interfaces that are new to the stakeholders, then this is a great technique for agreeing what needs to happen and uncovering further requirements. Storyboarding can include sketches to depict actions, interface screens, thoughts or emotions. It is less abstract than some of the techniques and allows discussion through the experience and whether there is anything else required to improve it.

REASONS FOR USING STORY BOARDS

Story boards are powerful tools for helping stakeholders understand their requirements and complement both use cases and user stories. Storyboarding enables the stakeholders to walk through the solution and to agree it together.

PUTTING TOGETHER A STORY BOARD

It involves drawing out on paper the different activities, what they contain and how they flow from one scenario to another. It is important when using story boards that they don't look like the finished product. If they do, the stakeholders may then not focus on the functionality and may have false expectations that the product is finished.

You can use pen and paper, sticky notes and cardboard boxes and even play the scenario out using role play. Discussions can include prioritization and help agree iterations of the product. The data, buttons and links to other pages can all be planned out if including interface screens used as part of the solution.

EXAMPLE

Storyboarding can be a powerful persuasion technique. I had a conflict where IT wanted to push through a solution that the business didn't agree with. The business stakeholders feared that the solution being suggested would be too complicated for their customers and cause problems. I wanted to get the functional requirements signed off but had one set of stakeholders or the other refusing to sign off the document unless they had their way. Creating a story board enabled the solution to be walked through and helped to get both sets of stakeholders more comfortable with the proposals, which enabled me to obtain approval.

Traditional table format

WHAT IS THE TRADITIONAL TABLE FORMAT?

This approach lists each of the capabilities required of the solution in a structured table format. Like the format of the business requirements given in Chapter 5, this table formatting has a unique reference number, short title, longer description, priority, source and rationale. It sets out all the functionality required.

The short title should look to group similar functional requirements together where there is a common solution. Functional requirements form part of detailing how the solution will work based on the business requirements. If there are different solutions, then this should be separated out and clearly labelled.

I would recommend creating a separate document for any solutions that are to be handled manually without a system. This will help the business to prepare and understand the responsibilities for the areas it needs to implement. Likewise, if there are separate system solutions that are required then these may warrant being in separate documents if they need different audiences to action them.

REASONS FOR USING THIS TECHNIQUE

Unlike the other techniques covered this does not provide analysis for eliciting requirements very easily. This is therefore a better technique to use once you have applied other techniques first to elicit requirements and use this for documenting afterwards. It is important not to populate the table using this method too soon. Prior to this technique you may wish to use business process modelling, use case models or casual use cases.

This technique makes it easy for traceability purposes, because each requirement can be visited in turn and checked to see whether it has been satisfied. This can be from a development perspective, when reviewing test scripts or test results, for example. However, a drawback is that a table may not make it easy to see whether anything has been missed out.

How do you deal with global non-functional requirements?

Non-functional requirements are requirements that the solution must meet to ensure the quality or the IT-related constraints of the organization. This section focuses on what are known as global non-functional requirements.

'Global' means they apply to the whole solution and across multiple functional requirements. In most projects there will be non-functional requirements related to just one or two requirements. They are documented in the acceptance criteria for user stories and in the special requirements if using use cases.

If you don't build in the global non-functional requirements to your solution you may find the product unusable. Here is a list of examples:

- The solution may not perform in a way that is acceptable to the users.
- The solution may not be available when required.
- The solution may be impossible to implement because it doesn't meet the requirements of the IT business area.
- It may be impossible for other systems to send data to, or receive data from, the new solution.
- If there is a major incident and the system goes down, you could lose all the data and not get them back.

Identifying global non-functional requirements

Global non-functional requirements must start being collated as early as possible. Some of them may be scattered in existing IT governance documents, in contracts and in existing service level agreements. This can make them difficult to identify, because stakeholders may feel that the work has already been done. In other ways this can make the collation process easier, because something is already documented.

I have listed below the main categories of non-functional requirements. Some of these will come from your business stakeholders, whilst others come from IT stakeholders. Ideally these would be set up as a standard set of NFRs that could be applied to any project. They could then be used as a starting point for each project.

As a rule, they should be written to follow the NICE checklist:

- Negotiable: They need to be negotiated and agreed between all stakeholders.
- Independent: They make sense read on their own without having to refer to other NFRs.
- Context: They are appropriate for the context of the solution and environment.
- Evaluated: They can be checked for feasibility and are testable.

You will notice that some of the non-functional requirements are quite technical. The reason I advocate them being elicited and collated by the business analyst is that the non-functional requirements need to be negotiated between the business and IT.

PERFORMANCE REQUIREMENTS

Performance requirements are about how fast the system or data need to respond to an interaction with a user. The impact of not meeting the performance requirements is that if the end users think it takes too long then they may not use it. Performance requirements are primarily collated from finding out about end user and business expectations, existing performances and industry standards.

The main three types of measurements are the following:

- Response times: It is important to understand how fast the business needs the new solution to perform. What response times does it need and who is the end user? If the solution is a website that customers need access to, you may want to obtain statistics on what the current performance is to ensure it isn't impacted or you may want to look at whether there are any industry standards that can be applied. If the end users are internal, what response times do they expect? It is important to make sure the requirements specified are measurable so that success can be measured. This is important for testing that the criteria have been met.

  – Example: A response time to load a web page to be less than 5 seconds.

- Processing times: These are needed if the solution requires someone to process something. For example, if asking a third party to collect, transform, map, validate and store some data then you may want to specify how long this should take.

  – Example: A maximum of a week is required from receipt of files to process completion.

- Query and reporting times: If a user action consists of retrieving a query to get back some data, then there may be a need to break down response times into categories depending upon the size of the query.

  – Example: Complex queries can be run overnight and the results be available the next day; simple queries must be completed within a few minutes.

CAPACITY REQUIREMENTS

Capacity requirements provide details to ensure the solution can cope with the volumes of data or users who are expected to use it in the immediate term and the future. The impact of not identifying capacity requirements correctly is the solution not being able to cope with the volumes and either falling over or not meeting the performance requirements. The capacity requirements will be obtained from investigating the volumes with the business and IT. There may already be reports on existing volumes and trend analysis.

There are four main areas of consideration for capacity requirements. These are:

- Volumes: The solution and the technology to support the solution must be designed around the volumes expected. If the solution contains amounts of data that need to be stored, then this will need to be sized. The impact if this isn't done is that performance times will be affected and there will be additional costs to buy more hardware to increase the solution's capacity. This is particularly important when writing requirements for external suppliers, as they will not be able to provide costs without it.

  – Example: There are an estimated 20,000–60,000 documents to be uploaded for the documentation store over a period of five years.

- Scalability: The volumes and number of users who need to be considered in the future must be estimated. This could include annual growth estimates or estimates for a three- or five-year period. This will help to ensure the solution can cope with the growth demands and doesn't fall over after a year.

  – Example: The number of users is estimated to grow at 10 per cent a year.

- Number of users: The total number of users who will be using the product needs to be established. This is to help ensure that the right number of licences are supplied for a product, which will impact costs. It will also help measure the success criteria that the product is designed to satisfy.

  – Example: There will be 20 users.

- Concurrent users: The number of users who will use the product at the same time needs to be established. A website might have requirements to cater for 20,000 users, but the number of concurrent users will be far smaller.

  – Example: The product will support five concurrent users.

USABILITY REQUIREMENTS

Usability requirements cover how the users will use the solution. The impact of not defining these could lead to the solution not being utilized because it is too difficult to use, which would alienate some stakeholders. Usability requirements can be understood by gaining an understanding of who will use the system and the impression that needs to be portrayed. Sources for this information might be the business stakeholder's knowledge of the users, user research and existing branding guidelines or creative designs. It might also be possible to get a list of existing users if you are amending a current system from IT stakeholders.

There are four main areas of consideration for usability requirements. These are:

- Look and feel standards: These need to be measurable. The way to do this might be to relate them to corporate branding or styles that need to be adhered to. In terms of websites there are standards that can be referred to. The World Wide Web Consortium (W3C) sets international standards at different levels that evidence different levels of accessibility.

  - Example: The solution website must conform to Web Content Accessibility Guidelines Level AA.

- User skill levels: The skill level required of users may need to be specified to explain what is required of the solution. For example, if the user skill level required is to have no knowledge of query languages then it becomes clear that any query solution must adhere to this.

  - Example: The user will not need any knowledge of how to use any querying languages.

- Error messages: Consideration might be given to setting out a list of meaningful error messages that should replace any system error codes.

  - Example: Error messages presented must be accompanied by sufficient meaningful information.

- Help facilities: The help facilities required need to be set out. For example, does additional help information need to be provided at field level on forms? Are dedicated help pages required? Are chat bots required?

  - Example: The user must be able to get information to explain each item of data that needs to be populated.

ARCHIVING REQUIREMENTS

Questions need to be asked about how long data need to be kept and at what point they can be archived or deleted. There are several reasons for this. Data use up space, which comes at a cost, so clearing data that are no longer required will help maintain performance and reduce the need to keep buying memory. It will also help maintain the performance of returning results from the users querying the data. The more data that have to be queried the longer it will take to return the results. There are also regulatory reasons why data shouldn't be kept longer than necessary. The compliance department if you have one will need to be engaged to check regulatory implications such as the General Data Protection Regulation (GDPR).

There is a difference between archiving and deleting data. Archiving means that the data can be retrieved again at some point if required. This may take longer to get depending upon how it is archived but provides the reassurance that it could be retrieved if necessary. Deleting the data is permanent. Requirements can be established from asking the business users how long they will need to use the data for and speaking to data governance and compliance to find out the policies on data retention.

Areas of consideration for archiving requirements include:

- Data retention and archiving: If the solution stores data then the different types of data need to be specified along with the amount of time each type needs to be kept and whether it needs to be archived. It is also worth specifying timescales and criteria for how archived data are retrieved if ever required.
  - Example: Customer data need to be kept for as long as a customer remains a customer. When a customer ceases to be a customer then all the related data should be kept for seven years and then archived.
- Data deletion: The archiving requirements need to set out when the data can be physically deleted so that they can no longer be retrieved.
  - Example: There are no deletion requirements; all data should be archived indefinitely so they can be retrieved again if required.

AUDITING REQUIREMENTS

Data or user actions can be audited. This means being able to find out who has changed something, when and what they did. It enables traceability so as to be able to find out what has happened if a change must be investigated. These requirements may come from users, who will be administrators of the system when they need to investigate why something has changed, or they may be part of security or IT standards.

Areas of consideration for archiving requirements include:

- Data: It is necessary to set out what needs to be audited. It could be important to know every bit of data that is changed, or the data to be audited could be very specific. It depends on why you need to know if there have been changes to the data. For example, in relation to business critical data values there could be a need to understand previous values in the event of a query or mistake. There also needs to be clarity on what should be captured as part of the audit. In addition to the previous and new values there may be a desire to capture who has made the change and when. This would then provide the ability to understand the source of the change to check its validity if required.

  - Example: To have an audit of what has changed, when and by whom.

- Timescales: A decision is required on the time period to retain the data for auditing. This will vary depending upon how often the data are expected to change and how far back the business might want to go.

  - Example: Audit files should be kept for a period of 12 months.

AVAILABILITY REQUIREMENTS

It is necessary to establish how much time the system needs to be available to its users. This is to ensure the system is up when it is required and to allow time for maintenance. Requirements will need to come from the business and IT.

Areas of consideration for availability requirements include:

- Hours of operation: The availability requirements should set out the hours the system needs to be available. If it is an internal system, the hours between 8 am and 5 pm may suffice. If it is an external system such as an internet that can be used by customers any time of day and on a global scale, the requirement might be that it needs to be 24/7.

  - Example: To be available 24/7 apart from agreed maintenance windows that will be agreed in advance.

- Maintenance plans: Consideration must be given as to whether agreed down time can be provided. There is a strong chance that maintenance on the system will need to be done by whoever is looking after it to ensure efficient working and to do any upgrades or back-ups. This may mean taking the system down. It is important that this is agreed to if necessary and that the timing is chosen that will have the least impact on the business. To understand this, you will need to find out from the business what the peak times of usage will be. This may mean looking at the usage expected throughout the whole year and avoiding peak periods. In specifying the availability requirements, a percentage may be specified as a service level agreement for agreed up time.

- Example: To meet a 99.8 per cent product availability requirement of agreed up time. This includes end to end system availability of all software, hardware and communications interfaces between the system and ancillary systems.

- Operation locations: The availability requirements should set out whether there is a difference in availability requirements between different locations.

- Example: The solution should be available from all approved organizational locations, including remotely via supported methods.

SECURITY REQUIREMENTS

Security requirements set out what needs to be protected and the level of security required to protect the organization's systems and data. They are essential for protecting customer data and company data and ensuring no one ends up being able to access data they shouldn't be able to see. Security breaches could lead to stolen data, ransom demands, loss of reputation and large fines. These requirements can be obtained from several sources such as IT security, business stakeholders and security policy documentation.

Areas of consideration for security requirements include:

- User access: Different parts of the system may require different levels of access, or there could be a mixture of public and more restricted areas. This all needs to be set out. There may be a desire to have rules around dormant accounts or time-out settings if the system hasn't been used for a time period.

- Example: Users will be locked out if they enter the incorrect password more than three times.

- User access roles: All the roles and the different levels of access need to be identified. The different roles may impact what a user can see and do. It is important to make sure these requirements can be measured.

- Example: It must be possible to assign users different access permissions, such as read only, read–write or administration privileges.

- Authentication: There are different methods for how users can be authenticated, with varying different levels of security. They will vary depending upon how secure the application needs to be and the level of vulnerability it has. Security requirements may need to consider the criteria and format a password may require, for example number of characters or use of alpha, numeric and special characters. Multi-factor authentication is an additional level of security if the system is to access confidential or sensitive data. For single-factor authentication, users provide a password. For two-factor authentication, they provide a password and need to possess something else. In banking, users are often asked for an additional piece of information or sent a text message with a code to enter. Single sign-on is another option where users have access and regularly log on to more than one system and it is preferred that they only enter in their information once. This will be common for internal IT systems where a user already has a Windows login password that they must use.

  - Example: The password must be eight characters long and contain alpha and numeric characters and a special character.

- Data storage: The security requirements need to set out how the data can be stored. Do any of the data need to be encrypted, which data, to what standard of encryption and when? The security may vary depending upon whether the data are at rest or in transit and where they are located. This is important if third parties are going to be hosting the data, as there will need to be confidence in their data leakage controls and how they prevent data being accidentally shared if hosted in a multi-tenant environment.

  - Example: Data stored in a multi-tenant environment must be segregated.

- Infrastructure: There may be constraints around infrastructure for security reasons, such as appropriate malware, cyber and network perimeter defences. There may also be requirements to consider for ensuring that the technologies used are regularly updated to the latest versions to keep up to date with the latest security threats.

  - Example: The server should have high availability. This is to ensure minimal down time if a piece of infrastructure fails.

BACK-UP AND RECOVERY REQUIREMENTS

It is necessary to ensure data are backed up and can be recovered in the event of an incident. Back-up and recovery requirements set out how long the business can manage without the system and how up to date the data need to be. Requirements will vary depending upon how often the data are updated and how important they are to the business. Requirements need to be obtained from the business and IT stakeholders, to ensure feasibility from both points of view.

Areas of consideration for back-up and recovery requirements include:

• Recovery time objective and recovery point objective: A recovery time objective (RTO) is the maximum time targeted for restoring a system after a disaster or disruption. Any longer than the time specified will lead to repercussions. This will depend upon the nature of the system, how often it is used and the impact to the business if it is unavailable. A recovery point objective (RPO) relates to the age of the back-up when restoring a system after a disaster or disruption. This will depend upon how often the system and the data in it change and how important it is for them to be up to date.

– Example: The recovery time objective (RTO) will be a maximum of 6 hours.

• Back-up frequency: It needs to be set out how often back-ups should be performed, the method used, and how and where the back-ups are stored. How long the back-ups should be retained is another consideration.

– Example: Weekly back-ups will be retained for three months.

IMPLEMENTATION REQUIREMENTS

These are design constraints that are based on existing technology and systems in the organization. If a company already has a significant invest-ment in one type of technology, there may be limited benefit in changing this. There will often be an IT enterprise strategy, and it is important to establish these requirements from speaking with enterprise architects. Solution architects will also be able to provide guidance.

Areas of consideration for implementation requirements include:

• Compatibility for inputs and outputs: The system may need to interface with data files or data from other systems. There may be constraints around this that will need to be specified. If they are not specified it might then lead to not being able to import data into or export data out of the system, which could make it unusable.

- Example: The system will be designed in a manner that permits customer data to be uploaded in bulk.

• Hardware constraints: Hardware is the physical elements of technology, such as computers, memory, CPU and monitors. It is basically all the different components of a computer. The chances are that hardware will already exist in your organization and this will cause limitations on what a new solution needs to use.

- Example: The organization operates hardware (both client and server) that is based upon Intel X86 architecture, both 32 bit (X86-32) and 64 bit (X86-64). The system will be fully compatible with hardware that is based upon this microprocessor architecture.

• Software constraints: Software runs on a computer to make it function. Again, your organization may have constraints on the type of software that can be used.

- Example: The organization's application servers presently operate on a Microsoft Windows Server 2008 R2 implementation. The system will be designed and implemented in a manner that supports compliance with this operating system.

SUPPORT REQUIREMENTS

Support requirements set out what is required to support the new solution. If an incident happens, a change is required or something needs to be escalated, there needs to be something in place to deal with it, along with timescales to resolve it that suit the business. The requirements will be obtained from a mixture of what is already in place, what the business needs and an agreement of how to resolve the difference if needed.

Areas of consideration for support requirements include:

• Incident management: This is where you can set out what needs to happen and be available if any issues or requests need to be raised. This could be along the lines of a service desk with the hours they need to be available to receive these. Priority level and definitions for each type of incident are required so that each incident raised can be categorized and responded to accordingly.

- Example: The solution provider will create a service desk that is available between 8 am and 6 pm (normal business days) to allow for any issues – or requests – to be raised and managed.

- Change management: Requirements around change management for handling requests to make future changes should be specified.
  - Example: A change management process needs to be in place to deal with changes.
- Service levels: Service levels need to be established to set out requirements for target response and resolution times. These will vary depending upon the priority and definitions set out under incident management (see above). There may also be requirements about how incidents are raised, and the process involved.
  - Example: Target response and resolution times will be within three business days.
- Escalation management: The purpose is to set out the escalation management process and who the key contacts will be. It is advisable to set out different escalation levels with different definitions and contacts.
  - Example: Level 1 escalation is to the service desk manager, level 2 to the vendor service manager, level 3 to the service delivery manager, level 4 to the head of managed service and level 5 to the operations director or CEO.
- Demarcation of support responsibilities: This is relevant if there are different third parties and an internal team providing support. It may be necessary to make it clear who will be responsible for what.
  - Example: Set out the responsibilities of the system integrator.
- Service management: To cover any service reporting and data that are required.
  - Example: Service improvements will be actively managed and reviewed through the request, problem and change management processes, and project/programme management processes for major business change.

EXAMPLE

It is very important that NFRs are negotiated to ensure they meet the needs of the business, are feasible from an IT perspective and are worth the cost associated with meeting them. But there will be trade-offs. For example, I once worked on a project where the business requested that it have the new system available 24 hours, 7 days a week. The IT department pointed out that it didn't offer that type of service for any other solution it was responsible for and that it normally took all the systems down nightly. The business request could be met, but it would come at a high cost. I had to establish the reasons why the business stakeholders wanted to access the system outside office hours and how often. It turned out that it was because there were sometimes requests from the regulator where data had to be retrieved from the system in a short turnaround time, which often led to the staff in the team working late. This happened on average two to three times a year. We were able to agree to have the system available for the same hours as the other internal systems but for there to be a manual process agreed to keep the system up on request.

How do you adapt requirements for commercial off the shelf packages?

Definition of commercial off the shelf packages and benefits

Commercial off the shelf packages (COTS) are pre-developed solutions that can be bought as a package and sold to a mass market. These packages have a large appeal because they enable businesses to buy something with most of the functionality required at a much lesser cost than that of building a solution from scratch. If the same product has been sold to multiple organizations then it can be interpreted as being tried and tested, which reduces the risk of poor quality. It also makes it faster to implement, because it just needs to be installed and configured.

Over time the company that has created the COTS may consider customer feedback and release new versions of the software with improvements that can be rolled out. If organizations use a package for similar purposes, they will often have similar requirements. This gives reassurance, because there will be future demands from companies for newer versions of the software that will evolve in line with the demands of the business. Companies that sell COTS products will often help, if required, in installing and configuring the software. They will often provide aftercare services to aid the organization with using the product and be able to answer questions on best practice from their experience of their customers.

Challenges with eliciting and documenting requirements

Obtaining system requirements for a custom-built product means that the product can be designed and built exactly as documented. With COTS products you are much more restricted. If you are too specific with your system requirements you may end up having no products that fit the criteria. A common saying when a decision is made to buy a COTS product to meet requirements is that the 'organization must adapt over adopt'. This means the business may have to change its processes to make the product work for it.

There is the possibility that not all the requirements can be met. An understanding is therefore required of what needs must be met by the software and what can be dropped if necessary. Cost savings may be possible by not needing a team of architects, developers and testers. However, if the COTS product needs to interface with other internal systems then these resources may still be required. Each organization will also have its own IT policies and strategy that will influence the non-functional requirements. So there will also still be a need to balance and negotiate these between the business and IT, along with an increased priority to understand their importance if trade-offs need to be considered.

Approach for eliciting and documenting requirements when the intended solution approach is COTS

The outcome of eliciting and documenting requirements is normally to feed them into a request for proposal (RFP). This is a document owned by procurement and gets sent off to a list of suppliers, which will then bid for the work based on what their COTS packages offer. In the next section I will describe more about the RFP and procurement process. This section covers what business analysis is required and how the approach may be slightly different.

BUSINESS NEEDS AND BUSINESS REQUIREMENTS

When eliciting requirements for a COTS solution approach, the process and techniques used begin in a similar way. You start with understanding the problems and opportunities. You use interviewing techniques and analyse documentation to understand what the business wants, and the inputs and outputs required. You document the business processes to ensure the same understanding. This is needed to get an idea of which processes the COTS package must support and will help afterwards in analysing the feasibility of altering the business processes if required.

SOLUTION REQUIREMENTS

The focus of the solution requirements should be: interfaces – inputs and outputs; reporting; functionality – features; non-functional requirements; priorities; and evaluation criteria.

- Interfaces: Inputs will allow the ascertaining of what data need to be received by the COTS package and how. Some considerations include: Is a graphical user interface required to enter data that users must manually type in and update? Do files need to be uploaded and how often? Do other systems need to interface directly with the COTS package and how often? To obtain the details about the interfaces and the data that need to go into the COTS system, input is needed from an IT architect and the business. The business stakeholders may have forms they can provide you with to show what data need to be entered. Electronic files may already exist that can be viewed to see what data need to go across. A business domain model or an entity data diagram can be used to highlight what data need to be imported from other systems. Equally data may need to go from the COTS system to other systems. Requirements around what data there are and where they should go will need to be analysed. Business rules will need to be understood around what needs to happen to the data and whether the data must be transformed before they are recorded in the COTS system. To enable costs to be understood, data volumes and sizes also need to be included in the analysis.

- Reporting: Reporting could be considered part of the outputs. Detail is required on what the reports need to be able to achieve, the number of them and who completes the reporting. It is possible that the business will be unable to define all the reports it wants, and the COTS provider may offer consultancy to help define the reports. Therefore, only enough information is required to give confidence that the COTS product can provide the type of reports required and enough to understand about the costs. To do this you may need to specify the number of reports, together with an indication of the size and complexity of each one.

- Functionality – features: The features required can be set out in a use case model along with a description providing more detail on what needs to happen. Some of the business processes identified may be required features of the product.

- Non-functional requirements: Non-functional requirements are among the most important parts of COTS analysis, because they set out the constraints that the software must meet. If the software cannot support the number of users required or is too costly then it may be considered unsuitable. The software must also be compatible so that it is able to create the interfaces required with other systems.

- Priorities and evaluation criteria: One of the most difficult challenges with writing the requirements designed to feed into an RFP is agreeing the evaluation criteria. If you are involved with defining these criteria, it is very important that you understand the priority of each of the inputs, outputs, reports, features and non-functional requirements to the evaluation assessment. Each vendor that replies to the RFP will be setting out how it can meet each of your requirements and providing a cost of doing so. Comparing each vendor and deciding which one is best will be partly down to how well a vendor can meet these requirements.

What is involved in the procurement process and how can business analysis help?

Definition and process

A request for proposal is written when work or a product is required from outside the organization. It could be to find a commercial off the shelf package as described previously or it could be to provide a service. This document is a way to state the requirements so that other companies can bid for the work with an understanding of the business needs. There is then a process to evaluate the responses. This document is normally owned by procurement. The team for putting the proposal together will typically consist of procurement, a business analyst, a solution architect, an enterprise architect and business representatives who are decision makers and those who will be using the service or system.

Sometimes a request for information (RFI) is sent out first before an RFP. This is much more informal and just outlines some of the needs at a much higher level. Suppliers may then express an interest and present back their offerings. This helps with understanding more about what is available and provides an opportunity for both parties to ask questions. The request for proposal follows this with more information to allow the third parties to understand more detail of what services are required, sets out the structure of the response, which must allow comparisons between the third parties, and asks the supplier to quote a cost. Depending upon how well the suppliers score they may then be invited back to discuss their responses in more detail.

In addition, there must be an agreement within the team involved with the selection process on the evaluation criteria and the method for scoring. This is to allow each response to be compared in the same way to make it easier to pick the best one. Business analysis involvement is to help the business define its business requirements, populate the related sections in the RFP, define questions for the third party and identify the evaluation criteria.

The RFP details sent out are considered in the following subsections.

Covering letter

The covering letter is normally written by procurement. It sets out the background of the organization the third party will be responding to, a summary of the service/product required, and the process and timelines for responding.

RFP

You should write the requirements in the RFP as business requirements following the principles and guidelines provided in Chapter 5. Also include interfaces, reporting, features and non-functional requirements if relevant. This enables the responses to explain how the supplier will meet each requirement. Make sure you group the requirements to make it easier to phrase the corresponding questions. The non-functional requirements may be structured slightly differently to those described when writing for internal use. Some companies writing an RFP prefer to explain their current set-up and ask the company expressing an interest to answer how it would meet this set-up rather than being too prescriptive. This has the added benefit of making visible the different answers provided by each vendor and enables an assessment of their level of maturity.

The more technical parts of the RFP and some of the non-functional requirements will be written by the IT architects.

Questions for third parties

There are questions you want the third party to respond to based on their reading of the detail in the RFP and covering letter. On receiving the responses each reviewer will analyse how well each third party has answered each of the questions. It is worth also requesting that a status of fully met, partially met or cannot meet is provided alongside each answer.

The questions will vary depending upon whether the request is about providing consultancy, support, customized development or an out of the box solution. It will also vary depending upon the evaluation criteria agreed. The questions will need to relate back to the sections and detail provided in the RFP. The idea is that the third parties will read the RFP and respond to how they will meet the detail in it by answering the questions.

CASE STUDY

Dream Phones decides it wants a new website to help customers buy and trade their phones online. It hasn't got the expertise to do this in-house, so it wants to send out an RFP to see whether other companies would be interested in doing this for it.

Here is a sample of some of the categories and questions it might ask:

1 Project methodology.

   a. What is your project methodology approach?

   b. Why is it appropriate?

2 Project approach.

   a. What is your systems requirements gathering approach?

   b. What is your development approach?

   c. What is your communication approach?

   d. What is your approach to testing and what documentation will you produce?

   e. How do you propose to provide the end user training?

   f. Does your approach fit with the key milestones set out?

3 Solution proposal against requirements.

   a. Please set out how you propose to enable our customers to provide their old phone details.

   b. Please set out how you propose to enable our customers to obtain quotes for their mobile phones.

    c. Please set out how you propose to enable our customers to search for a new mobile phone.

    d. Please set out how you propose to enable our customers to provide customer details and payment.

    e. Please set out how you propose to enable marketing to monitor trends.

    f. Please set out how you propose to enable marketing to target and send marketing messages.

4 Technical.

    a. Describe the systems architecture for your proposed solution.

    b. Describe how you propose to integrate with our other systems.

    c. What system requirements are required to meet your proposed solution?

    d. What is your auditing capability and how does it compare with the auditability requirements?

    e. How can you guarantee response times as specified in the performance requirements?

    f. Can the proposed solution support the availability requirements?

    g. What are the constraints to scalability?

5 Support.

    a. Please propose a business as usual support/operational model appropriate for the solution.

    b. How long is the warranty period and what does it cover?

    c. What is your disaster recovery process?

6 People.

    a. What team structure are you proposing throughout the lifecycle of the project? Please provide a diagram to illustrate this.

    b. What are the roles and who are the project members you would involve from your company to work on building our new website?

    c. Who will have overall responsibility and accountability for this work within your organization?

    d. Will staff be dedicated to the project or will they also have another workload to consider?

    e. Who will be working full time and part time at our office? Who will be working from other locations and are they on-shore or off-shore?

    f. How will your project structure interact with our organization?

    g. Provide professional biographies of the key members in the team.

    h. What experience has your company had in producing solutions of this nature before in this sector?

7 Security.

    a. Please provide responses that consider the requirements as laid out in the security requirements.

    b. Please reference any appropriate certifications, standards and industry best practices that you hold, conform to or consider relevant to your responses for the services that you are interested in providing.

    c. How do you plan to conform to data-related regulations like GDPR etc?

8 Commercial costs.

    a. Please provide licences/subscription costs and a quote for a length of one year, three years and five years. Include detail on the pricing model, for example per user, block of users, fixed etc.

    b. Please provide hardware costs if applicable.

    c. Please provide hosting costs.

    d. Please provide consultancy costs. Please break costs down by job types, rates etc for each use case.

    e. Please provide your support costs and a quote for a length of one year, three years and five years.

    f. What are your assumptions behind these cost estimates?

9 Commercial terms and conditions.

    a. Is the charging model proposal fixed or capped?

    b. What are your contractual terms?

How do you evaluate responses from software providers?

Evaluation process

During the vendor assessment process, a business analyst might be part of the evaluation committee, which consists of the people who will provide the scoring for each of the vendors and be part of the discussions about which one should be selected. A business analyst might help with putting the evaluation criteria together based on what is important. Individuals may score individually but then discuss the results to get a group consensus. Scoring may be based on the answers provided in the RFP and on presentations if the vendors are invited.

It is important to think about evaluation criteria other than how well the vendor responds to the questions. This is to assess how easy the third party would be to work with and whether it would be a compatible fit. During the internal evaluation discussions there will need to be conversations on the quality of the responses and presentations, whether the third party has understood what has been asked and the level of confidence in each one to deliver.

Once the evaluation criteria have been agreed then weightings should be assigned. This is because some evaluation criteria will be more important than others. Typically, the weighting range will be 1 to 5, with 1 for the least important criteria and 5 for the most important. Each score provided by each person in the evaluation committee or in the group total should be added up and multiplied by the weighting.

CASE STUDY

Dream Phones has now sent off the RFP and agreed the evaluation criteria and weightings shown in Table 6.3, which also gives a description of what needs to be considered for scoring. You will notice that each criterion has been given a weighting. It was decided that the technical requirements, business requirements and security were the most important criteria. Project methodology was thought to help with understanding whether the vendor would fit with the culture, but this wasn't as important as some of the other criteria.

Each of the questions sent out as part of the questionnaire was then associated with each of the evaluation criteria in Table 6.3 so the answers could be assessed against each of these categories.

TABLE 6.3 Evaluation criteria

Criterion	Description	Weighting (1–5)
Project methodology	Strength of project methodology recommendation compared with the organization's culture, suitability for the size of the project and industry best practice	1
Scope and project approach	Approach to gathering system requirements Approach to development Approach to communication Approach to testing Approach to training Approach to documentation Approach to fitting with key milestones	3
Technical	How well does the bidder meet the infrastructure requirements, alignment to strategy and architectural fit? To what degree does this proposal meet stated physical solution requirements (for hardware and/or software)?	5
Business requirements	How well does the bidder meet each of the business requirements?	5
Support	How well does the bidder meet the support requirements, including service desk and warranty period?	3
People	Does the bidder have the necessary skills and abilities to deliver this proposal? Is the resourcing structure appropriate? Does the bidder have a proven track record in this type of project? How much confidence do you have in the bidder? How easy do you think the bidder would be to work with?	3
Security	How well does the bidder meet the security requirements?	5
Commercial – costs	Are the costs clearly specified? How does the proposed price compare to (a) the planned budget and (b) other proposals?	4
Commercial – terms and conditions	Is the bidder willing to do a fixed or capped cost? Are the commercial terms and conditions provided reasonable?	4
TOTAL		

What are the approaches for agile projects?

Agile itself does not stipulate how to apply its principles. However, there are several frameworks that can be used that are tried and tested. I summarize some of these in this section. It is useful to have an awareness of them and be familiar with some of the terminology used. It is important to understand that these frameworks must be appropriate to the business context, as this can vary from project to project. What might be suitable in one situation might not be in another. Many companies adapt and combine these frameworks to make them suitable for themselves.

Scrum

This is a popular framework most associated with developing new software. It has defined roles, artefacts and standard events such as meetings. It is very process based.

ROLES IN SCRUM
Scrum master   This person will protect the team from being pulled off on to areas that do not directly relate to the work objectives required. These are called impediments and are recorded and monitored to keep them under control. The scrum master will also run the key meetings to ensure the meetings are kept on track and lessons are learnt throughout the project. The scrum master will track the progress of the work and report on it.

FIGURE 6.4 Scrum framework terminology

Roles	Artefacts	Meetings
Scrum master	Product backlog	Daily scrum
Product owner	Sprint backlog	Sprint planning
Team	Increments	Sprint review
		Sprint retrospectives
		Scrum of scrums

Product owner   The product owner will provide the vision of what needs to be built and will prioritize the list of the features required of the product. The product owner will own the product backlog (described under 'Artefacts' below). The product owner is responsible for the profitability of the product and will accept or reject the output of the work at the end of each sprint. The product owner is one person, not a committee, which helps to ensure decisions are made swiftly. The product owner must be senior enough to be able to make these decisions.

Team   This will be a cross-section of people with combined experience to actually do the work of delivering the software. The different disciplines that the team members might have been specialized in are not emphasized, but instead the members are asked to pull together to learn from each other and combine their expertise. The team is small, with no more than nine people. If there is a need to have more people on the project, then teams will be divided up to deliver different features of the system to keep the team size small. The team is responsible for estimating the size of the work, and success or failure is attributed to the whole team and not individuals.

ARTEFACTS

Product backlog   All the items to be worked on are stored in what is known as a product backlog. It contains everything that needs to be known about the product. It therefore covers the requirements, any changes, technical considerations, features and acceptance criteria, among others. The list is not fixed and can be added to throughout the whole length of the project. The contents of the product backlog are known individually as product backlog items. User stories are the most common approach for populating the product backlog.

Sprint backlog   This is created for each sprint. Sprints are iterations of work often two to four weeks in length. Work is only entered into a sprint if it is thought that an outcome can be shown at the end of it. Sprints are often numbered so that they can be easily referenced. Anyone can view the sprint backlog to see what it is expected will be delivered. Items for a sprint are obtained from the product backlog.

Increments   This is the work that gets delivered at the end of each sprint.

MEETINGS

Daily scrum   There is normally a daily scrum meeting with the whole team to discuss progress and any issues that need addressing. It should last no longer than 15 minutes in total and involves everyone standing up throughout the meeting and taking it in turns to speak. Each person in the scrum meeting answers three questions: What did I do yesterday? What am I doing today? Do I have any blockers preventing me from carrying out my work?

Sprint planning   Prior to a sprint the work is planned out with the whole team in what is called a sprint planning session. The team only commits to having the work placed in a sprint if it thinks the work is achievable in that amount of time. The product owner's contribution is to give the team the priority order so it can add the achievable items to the sprint in order of business value. The scrum master will facilitate the session to ensure everyone's voice is heard and the work is committed at the end of the session for the sprint.

Sprint review   At the end of each sprint the outcomes of the work are played back in a session called a sprint review. This is an informal session that encourages open feedback and where anyone in the organization who wants to be included can come along. It is the team's opportunity to present what it has achieved in the sprint according to what was planned in the sprint backlog.

Sprint retrospectives   The scrum master will facilitate retrospective meetings to assess with the team whether any improvements can be made to improve productivity. This helps with the concept of self-organizing and empowering teams. It is run after every sprint. All attendees can contribute and answer the three questions: What should we continue to do? What should we stop doing? What should we start to do?

Scrum of scrums   This is only applicable if several scrum teams have been created to deliver different features of a product. In addition to a daily scrum there will be a meeting for all the scrums, with one attendee from each scrum team so that all the scrum teams are represented. This is to ensure clarity over the whole product.

Kanban board

Work is tracked and monitored using what is called a Kanban board. There aren't any defined roles like those used in the scrum framework or planned sprints or iterations. Instead work progress is continually tracked through different statuses so work flows and is managed without overloading the development team. Whereas, in scrum, changes are not allowed, within a sprint changes can be made at any point on a Kanban board. The statuses provided are shown across the top horizontally from left to right. The statuses are typically product backlog, to do, in progress and completed, but these can vary depending upon what statuses the team thinks are most appropriate. The columns are then populated with all the different work that is needed for the team to do. The work is pulled through in priority order and will sit in the product backlog column until it is allocated to a team member to progress. When the team member has the capacity to work on it, he or she will move it to the in progress column before moving it to completed when finished. Sometimes the names of the team members are provided down the left so there is a visual record provided of who is working on what. Sticky notes are often used to make it easier to move the work across the Kanban board as it progresses.

Planning and progress meetings are held daily to ensure the work is being moved through, starting with the highest priority so that the team pulls it through according to the team capacity.

Extreme programming

The whole team must be co-located and sit together. This includes the business subject matter expert, who has knowledge of the requirements, business analyst, who will help the business subject matter expert with defining the requirements, developers, testers and other team members. The focus is on the quality of the code being developed.

Planning is based on what is to be achieved for each release and breaks down into delivery by iteration, which is a smaller timescale of normally two weeks. Results can then be viewed of what the programmers have

FIGURE 6.5 Kanban board

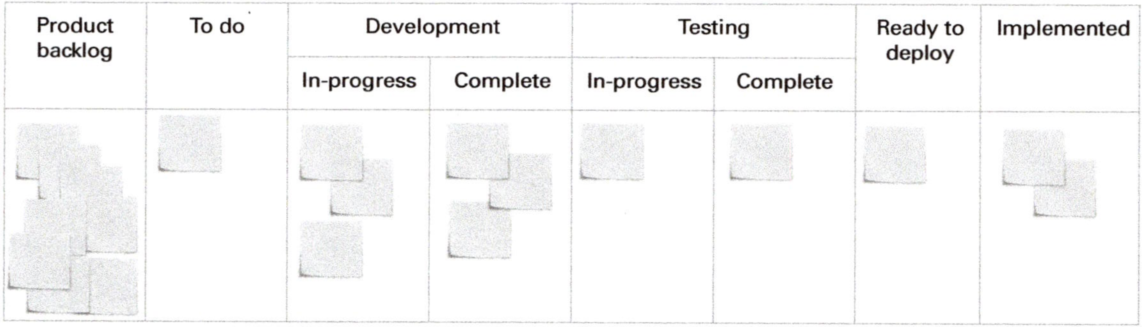

Product backlog	To do	Development		Testing		Ready to deploy	Implemented
		In-progress	Complete	In-progress	Complete		

completed at the end of it. Automated testing is very important for this framework, because it forms part of the acceptance criteria at the end of each iteration.

Programmers work in pairs throughout the whole development and sit at the same machine. This is thought to improve the outputs, because it means the code is continually being peer reviewed, so is likely to remove problems sooner.

Unified process

Unified process (UP) is sometimes seen as a halfway house between waterfall and agile. In UP, work is delivered in an iterative and incremental manner, but the number of times the work is revisited tends to be planned out in advance. This makes it less fluid than some of the other frameworks. It consists of four phases:

- Inception: This provides the project initiation tasks and identifies the vision, feasibility, resources and initial requirements. A release plan is then agreed.
- Elaboration: This sets out the requirements analysis and architecture required. The approach for the requirements and design is typically use cases. There will be a number of elaboration iterations that build on the use cases, often in conjunction with a prototype.
- Construction: This then develops the software based on the use cases from the elaboration phase.
- Transition: The aim is to conduct the activities that will release the solution into production.

Disciplined agile

This framework claims to take the best bits of other frameworks and provides more of a project end to end process. It doesn't focus just on software development, but has a strong focus on governance with staged gates.

It consists of three parts:

- Inception: This provides the project initiation tasks and identifies the vision, feasibility, resources and initial requirements. A release plan is then agreed.

- Construction: This creates work items, and work is carried out in iterations on the highest-priority items first from an iteration backlog. This is like scrum, but the term 'iteration' is used rather than the word 'sprint'. The aim is to produce a working piece of software at the end of each iteration, which is played back to obtain feedback, and to make continuous improvement changes. There is no specific recommended approach for documenting the work items.

- Transition: The aim is to conduct the activities that will release the solution into production.

EXAMPLE

I was able to reduce the timelines of a high-priority project that had an urgent deadline. It was estimated it would take 12 months using a waterfall approach. By changing the approach to agile I was able to get working software delivered in three months. This involved getting a team together from different areas of the business and developers from a third party, with the corporate customer accessible daily. We were able to break the work down and agree the items of the highest value first. We played back progress on a regular basis and were able to unblock issues quickly from having all the stakeholders in the meetings to get fast decisions and ownership of actions.

07

Managing requirements

Introduction

Once you have elicited and documented your requirements, it doesn't stop there. Requirements must be managed to ensure that they are agreed and kept up to date, that progress within a project aligns back to what was originally captured and that any changes are handled effectively.

It is not always easy to get your stakeholders to read documentation they have been given relating to requirements. They have their day jobs competing with the time they have available for the project. This chapter will provide you with tips to ensure you get stakeholders' time and suggestions for how to make what you produce easier for them to read and understand.

When requesting approval for documentation, stakeholders will often need time to review the material and an avenue to provide feedback to incorporate any changes or clarify their understanding. For a business analyst, it can be overwhelming if you are receiving feedback from several stakeholders, trying to incorporate suggestions and handling different opinions. In this chapter you will be shown best practice to manage this and provide a clear audit trail of what is incorporated, from whom and where push-back has been required.

Documentation used as a basis for working towards the solution must be approved by representative stakeholders. This is to ensure agreement before more money is spent. It would be costly to produce something for the stakeholders only for it not to be what they asked for. Different stakeholders may also have varying views, so it is important to get these aligned early on; otherwise there is a risk that the areas of the business will never accept the end solution or use the solution or that important functionality will be missed out.

Each requirement provided has time and cost associated with investigating, designing and implementing. Therefore, requirements must be prioritized, as it is necessary to know what can be delayed given constraints of time and budget. Further delays would be caused if you then had to go back and work it out later.

Business analysis involvement is necessary throughout the lifespan of a project. This is for a number of reasons, including to ensure that each deliverable traces back to what the project sets out to do. Traceability can be ensured through several different approaches. These will be explained along with methods for doing each. There may be changes as projects progress owing to the development of a better understanding of what is required, unplanned changes due to internal or external factors, new requirements or requirements being made redundant. Regardless, there needs to be a process to handle the changes, as there is no use ploughing on with delivering something that will be out of date and could have been fixed earlier.

Questions answered in this chapter for managing requirements

- How do you get stakeholders to read your documentation?
- How do you handle stakeholders' feedback when they have reviewed your documentation?
- How do you get your documentation signed off?
- How do you prioritize requirements?
- What is traceability and why is it important?
- How do you conduct traceability?
- How do you manage changes to requirements?

How do you get stakeholders to read your documentation?

Early engagement

Engaging stakeholders early on and taking them on the journey through building up your requirements documentation make the process easier. It is much harder to get people up to speed if they are involved late, because they may end up asking questions that have already been answered.

Using diagrams

Making use of diagrams will help stakeholders to read your documentation. It is faster and easier to read a diagram on a page than it is to write about the same thing, which can take several pages. Diagrams are also less ambiguous, so it is easier to spot if something isn't portrayed accurately. Some people will also respond better to diagrams, because they will find it easier to think in pictures so will find interpretation easier. You will have a variety of stakeholders, so it is important to make your documents cater for the different types of thinking represented.

Grouping requirements

Always group the requirements by use case or by business process using the techniques described in some of the previous chapters. As a recap, use cases divide the work down into smaller manageable chunks and represent user end goals. Business processes represent a sequence of activities that take place to achieve a goal. Grouping the requirements will provide more structure, making documentation easier to read. It will also enable your stakeholders to focus on the requirements most relevant to them. A further benefit is that it will avoid accidentally duplicating requirements. It can sometimes be difficult to understand if the same requirement has been provided by different stakeholders but with different terminology used. Grouping will make this easier to spot and help streamline the focus of your requirements.

Organizing walkthroughs

Whenever you send out documentation for review, I would recommend setting up a walkthrough of the document. This ensures everyone is focused on walking through the document step by step and allows for questions at each stage. This helps enable understanding of any confusions or differences of opinion. It is also easier to resolve these with the stakeholders in the room than to try to deal with them afterwards.

Always document any outcomes from walking through the document, including changes, feedback and decisions. Send these out as minutes to all the parties involved. At the end of the meeting, if all the changes have been addressed, then ask and minute whether the document can be signed off based on what has been agreed. There is no point dragging out the time period for sign-off if it can be done in a shorter timeframe. You will need to ask whether stakeholders want to see the changes before signing-off or whether they will sign off based on the changes being included without a further review.

How to handle stakeholders' feedback when they have reviewed your documentation

Sending out documentation

When sending out documentation for review always accompany it with a feedback form. This feedback form allows stakeholders to record all their feedback in a standardized format that can be collated and responded to more easily. Receiving a document back with tracked changes or as a hard copy with scribbles on is harder to manage. This process also provides a traceable audit.

Feedback form structure

The feedback form should contain the following headings:

- 'Document and version for review';
- 'Name of reviewer';
- 'Date of review';
- 'Document reference from the reviewer';
- 'Feedback narrative from the reviewer';
- 'Feedback type – observation, question, change required from the reviewer';
- 'Feedback response narrative from the business analyst';
- 'Changes made to document as a result from the business analyst'.

Receiving and responding to feedback

Enforcing the use of this form is important. This will enable you to respond individually to each piece of feedback and to state whether you are going to change your document as a result or whether there are good reasons for not incorporating a change. If there is conflicting feedback between stakeholders, this method makes it easier to get the stakeholders in a room to see the conflicting feedback and to reach a consensus. It also makes it clear whether the people giving feedback expect you to do anything with their comments. Finally, it provides an avenue for you to state whether you have incorporated the changes as a result of the feedback and to explain instances where you haven't.

How do you get your documentation signed off?

Managing sign-offs

As part of managing requirements it is crucial that the stakeholders whose needs you are addressing agree to what is required and that you have captured it accurately. The stakeholders who will be involved with providing a solution also need to agree that the requirements are feasible, achievable and understood.

The best way to make sure of this is to obtain sign-off from each key representative. This provides an audit trail to prove the requirements were agreed and what was agreed. There only needs to be one representative from each business area where a signatory is required who provides sign-off. However, there can be others in business areas who can be classified as reviewers who check documentation before referring to the signatory in their business area.

The reason for not wanting too many signatories is so you don't have to chase too many signatures. Having one in each business area makes one person responsible for checking that colleagues agree, cutting down the effort for yourself. The signatory should also be the most senior person and therefore have the authority to check with the team.

Physical signatures are not necessary, as a confirmation by email will also provide the evidence you need. It is also less likely to be lost if stored electronically than a signature. If you do get signatures you can scan them in and store them centrally. When you send out a document ready for sign-off, always make it clear who the signatories are and provide a deadline to have responses by. When the deadline is approaching, send reminders by email. The day before the deadline, ring each of the signatories to check there are no problems with obtaining approval. On the day of the deadline or if there are missing responses, visit each person you have not heard from if possible.

Never do assumed sign-offs, where it is held that no response means sign-off is assumed. This is bad practice and is not recommended.

Use of caveats

If stakeholders haven't responded with an approval, it is important to ask if the lack of response is due to any concerns they have and if there is anything you can do to mitigate these concerns. If the concerns are outside of your control, then there might be a case for allowing approval with caveats. Caution should be used with this method, as the requirements should be completed before asking for sign-off. Caveats should not be used if stakeholders believe requirements are missing. However, if their concern is related to something outside your control then it will help put your stakeholders at ease if you make sure the concern is reflected in a log of risks, issues, dependencies or assumptions. It will also need to be added to the project central register.

Agile documentation

There is an emphasis in agile on working software over documentation, but there is still normally some type of documentation even if more lightweight. There is also still some form of approval, for example solution deliverables, such as user stories prior to development. Documentation will be created incrementally and continually, rather than as a one-off as it is in waterfall projects. The number of sign-offs is restricted to a small number of stakeholders who are responsible for the business outcomes.

The development team also must agree they have enough understanding of what is required. This is done through conversations, but there is normally something written down to agree what can be achieved in each iteration of work. To set expectations there is an agreement of a definition of what constitutes 'ready'. This explains the success criteria required to pull the work into an iteration and what level of information is needed, for example 'Does the solution need wireframes showing the layout of the screens prior to development, pictures to be used or another type of support?' There will be fewer hold-ups if this is all agreed with the teams in advance.

How do you prioritize requirements?

Importance of prioritizing

All requirements need to have a priority associated with them, and the priorities must not all be high. There can be a temptation for the business to give a priority of essential to all of its requirements because it thinks that is the only way to ensure they get completed. Equally, the IT department is often guilty of stating it will only deliver the high-priority requirements and ignoring those that are of a lesser priority.

This makes the job of business analysis much harder, because ensuring the priority is correct and acceptable for all stakeholders takes skill. The reason why requirements need to be prioritized is that there are always time and budget constraints. Ultimately, fulfilling every requirement often is not feasible in one phase. Understanding the priority enables swift action if there must be compromises. If you must go back to the business to ask for further decisions, then this will cause further delays.

Methods for prioritizing

The most common method for categorizing requirements into a priority is MoSCoW: Must have, Should have, Could have, Won't have. Each requirement needs to have one of these priorities assigned, and they must be agreed by all the stakeholders. This can be difficult, not just because of the fear of only getting ones that have been given a must rating but also because the stakeholders will have different viewpoints and agendas.

EXAMPLE

Must have

These are requirements without which the project would not be worth doing from day 1. They are integral to the success of the project. There are no feasible manual workarounds.

Should have

These are high-value requirements important for the success of the project. They are not as time-critical as the must category, and there are manual workarounds that could be enacted in the short term if not delivered on day 1.

Could have

These are requirements that it is nice to have. The project could still be a success without them, but they would be useful to have if time allowed.

Won't have

These are requirements that the business has accepted could be future requirements. I suggest you move these requirements to an appendix and not include them in the main requirements section if using a traditional table format in a business requirement document or solution requirements document. This will prevent any misunderstanding from those providing the solution if they do not notice the priority difference, but these requirements will still be visible enough to ensure they will be considered for future phases.

Techniques to support prioritization

QUOTAS AND SEQUENCING

Setting clear definitions for the business will help it prioritize the requirements. As a guide you could set a quota to allow only 60 per cent of the requirements to have a priority of must. Sharing this figure with the stakeholders will help them focus on what can be given a lower priority if necessary and make your life easier. If you have a good relationship with your stakeholders, get them to put the requirements in an ordered sequence first without considering the categories. This will help them with their decision making and to understand their rationale.

BUSINESS VALUE

There are other questions you can ask to help determine priority, for example asking how stakeholders would rate the requirement in terms of business value. This can encourage stakeholders to look at requirements from a different perspective. It may be a high priority to them, but in terms of value prompt them to understand they may be able to cope without it in the shorter term, pushing the priority down to a should or could. Therefore, it is important to go through the definitions of each category before asking the stakeholders to prioritize. Business value could relate to a number of factors, such as the amount of time it could save, accuracy and availability of information, reputational risk or treating customers fairly.

RATIONALE

Understanding the rationale provided for a requirement might provide clues as to whether it really is a must have. If the rationale is because it has already been done a certain way, then it is important to understand the reasoning behind it and whether it is still applicable for the project.

REGULATION

In some projects there may be more must have requirements if they relate to regulation. This is where business value might be low, but the requirements still must be implemented to avoid enforcement action or large fines.

TRACEABILITY

Priority can also be determined on whether each requirement traces back to the objectives of the project and the problem statement. If it doesn't then it is harder to justify a high priority or possibly even having it as a requirement.

AGILE-RELATED PROJECTS

Agile projects have a distinct advantage in prioritization because there is often a dedicated role, such as the product owner, used in the scrum framework described in Chapter 6. This is where one person is responsible for prioritizing the requirements in a backlog. Changes are allowed, so the order may change throughout the project as more and more information is known. This allows for business agility where requirements are re-prioritized to keep up with the pace of change.

What is traceability and why is it important?

Traceability is about making sure that, throughout the delivery of a project when implementing change, progress always relates back to what is expected and set out. As covered in previous chapters there are different levels of information obtained throughout the process for implementing change. A project lifecycle tends to go through the following phases: project initiation, business requirements, solution/system requirements, development, testing, implementation. Throughout this, traceability checks should be conducted. This is where checks are done to ensure each stage relates back to all the other stages (see Figure 7.1).

Alignment

In any project it is important to ensure the changes delivered relate back to the problems identified, business requirements and solution requirements. If they are not all aligned consistently throughout, then there is a danger of the project not achieving the needs originally set out and not achieving the benefits expected.

FIGURE 7.1 Planning the traceability approach

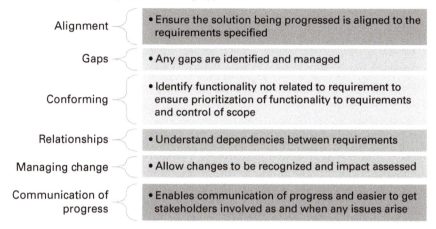

Alignment	• Ensure the solution being progressed is aligned to the requirements specified
Gaps	• Any gaps are identified and managed
Conforming	• Identify functionality not related to requirement to ensure prioritization of functionality to requirements and control of scope
Relationships	• Understand dependencies between requirements
Managing change	• Allow changes to be recognized and impact assessed
Communication of progress	• Enables communication of progress and easier to get stakeholders involved as and when any issues arise

SOURCE Helen Winter (2017) Planning the traceability approach, businessbullet.co.uk, 5 March.

Preventing gaps

Traceability is useful in making sure there are no gaps in a project. Common scenarios for gaps appearing include those where the requirements are difficult to understand, there are different stakeholders providing parts of the solution or the requirements are difficult to achieve. Therefore, it is very important for the business analyst to be involved throughout the whole of a project and not just at the requirements stage. As business analysts identify gaps they are best placed to make sure any issues causing a gap are identified and resolved.

If gaps are related to a misunderstanding of requirements, walkthroughs and answers to questions should be provided. If the solution subject matter experts have not provided complete coverage to meet all the requirements, the business analyst can get those responsible together to discuss who will provide ownership of the solution. Sometimes there are assumptions that another party will deal with a gap, but there needs to be a consensus taking into account the different impacts and where the solution is best placed. It is no use assuming the business can introduce a manual solution if the effect of it doing this would mean recruiting a huge team and this then costing more than providing a technical solution.

Conforming

Tracing progress back reaffirms that the requirement was needed in the first place to help prevent gold plating and scope creep. These are things that contribute to an increase in project costs.

> **EXAMPLE**
>
> Gold plating is when the solution provided exceeds the requirements and something cheaper and simpler would have been adequate. Scope creep is when additional requirements are introduced that were not originally identified, leading to solutions that are not needed and will never be used.

The project could be addressing requirements that were originally missed, which might appear positive, but then there is a danger that there hasn't been an assessment of how to introduce the change and an understanding of its impact. Traceability helps with the prioritization of requirements, because if they do not relate back to the biggest problems then their worth can be more easily challenged.

Relationships

There are often requirements that are interconnected and may depend on each other. For example, requirements to show outputs cannot be progressed unless the requirements to retrieve the data are made available first. Traceability allows all these types of requirements to be tracked and highlights if there are any hold-ups that may then prevent other requirements from being implemented.

Managing change

Any new requirements need to be carefully managed to ensure they do not get lost and still have traceability. This normally involves requirements being handled by a change request, which is described in more detail under 'How do you manage changes to requirements' later in this chapter.

Communication of progress

Traceability provides all stakeholders with a view of the progress and gives them comfort at each stage that their needs will still be met. It enables stakeholders to check they are happy with the outputs and helps them to prepare in advance for the changes that will impact them. If there are any issues preventing delivery, visibility is maintained and it is clear which requirements issues relate to. This enables business areas to prepare contingencies if necessary, provide further information to help if necessary or re-prioritize.

How do you conduct traceability?

Waterfall projects

Business analysts are normally best placed to pull together and track traceability because they are already familiar with the requirements and have already built up relationships with each of the types of stakeholders. They can help each set of stakeholders understand the requirements and problems that need to be resolved. They are also able to challenge and highlight any gaps.

Being responsible for traceability requires good relationships with the business subject matter experts, the solution subject matter experts including developers and architects, the project manager, the testers, the suppliers and so forth. As each stage progresses through the project lifecycle there must be a check each time considering multiple viewpoints.

One of the best ways to conduct traceability is to use an Excel spreadsheet. The use of multiple tabs allows the different viewpoints required to be created and catered for. The following are examples of the different viewpoints and the type of contents:

- Viewpoint 1 example: This provides a list of the problems and evaluation success criteria that the solution must meet. Each type of deliverable must relate back to these. The problems and success criteria are listed down the left-hand side, and the types of deliverables across the top. You will need to demonstrate and evidence that each deliverable has been checked. This could involve a tick or a reference number indicating where in the document it is addressed.

- Viewpoint 2 example: This checks that each type of deliverable relates back to the business requirements (see Figure 7.2 for an example). Each business requirement is listed down the left-hand side, and the deliverables are then listed across the top. A check is done that the solution requirements, any design documentation, development and testing relate back to the business requirements.

- Viewpoint 3 example: This could be related to the data requirements when data are a key element of a project and new data must be collated and shown. All the types of data expected are listed, and each piece of data is tracked to ensure delivery and testing.

- Viewpoint 4 example: This could relate to reporting or correspondence. Each piece of reporting or correspondence is tracked to ensure delivery and testing.

FIGURE 7.2 Traceability matrix

Business requirements										Delivery Approach				Testing strategy				Progress	
Reqts ref.	Category	Reqts description	Priority	Source doc.	Business benefit	Supportive docs to the business reqts doc	Solution delivery phase	Size of work (small, medium, large)	Method for meeting reqts	Scope	Out of scope	Solution doc.	Test scripts	Test update narrative	Testing signed off	Status	Last updated date	Status narrative	

This will help give the project team and business confidence they are getting what they want. However, they will not want to wade through all the detail provided in the spreadsheet. Thus, consider utilizing graphs and charts to summarize the progress and to highlight any risks of not achieving what is required. This information can be relayed back in regular team meetings.

Traceability in agile projects

SPRINT REVIEWS AND STATUS REPORTS

Documentation may be lighter owing to the emphasis on providing outcomes and this being a measure. However, there are techniques available to provide traceability. The project deliverables are captured in a product backlog, and frameworks such as scrum are placed in time box iterations known as sprints. Sprint reviews are then carried out at the end to track which items of delivery are accepted and which are not. To aid governance, status reports of each sprint can be produced. This will help show what wasn't delivered as planned. A status report will show the objectives of the sprint/iteration, which items on the backlog were expected to be delivered and what wasn't delivered and why.

VIEWPOINTS

Agile projects still need to start out having a vision. The high-level headings of the vision are identified as epics to show what needs to be covered, and this is then broken down into lower levels of detail, in user stories for example. Tasks are added to the user stories and tracked to ensure traceability. If this is all inputted into tracking tool software, then reports can be produced from it to show progress and traceability automatically without the use of a separate traceability matrix.

RELATIVE ESTIMATION, VELOCITY AND BURN-DOWN CHARTS

A popular method in agile for providing traceability is the use of burn-down charts, which were developed by Ken Schwaber. Burn-down charts provide visibility of the progress against an estimated product backlog. They can be used to measure velocity, which in agile is how much a team can deliver in a short time period referred to as a sprint or iteration. It is important to monitor velocity, because it recognizes that team performance can improve the more the team members self-organize and work together. Therefore, measuring velocity for each iteration and tracking it in a burn-down chart is important not just for measuring progress but also for predicting completion.

FIGURE 7.3 Fibonacci sequence

Story points can be used to measure velocity. Before velocity can be measured the product backlog has to be estimated. Story points are assigned first
by listing the contents of the product backlog in order of estimated size.
Teams will normally do this together in silence. This provides what is called
relative estimation. The teams will then need to group the items by size.
Consideration will be given depending upon complexity, risk, number of
unknowns and effort. The user stories are then assigned story points depending on whether they are smaller or larger. Story points are assigned to the
groups according to a Fibonacci sequence (see Figure 7.3).

The story points for all the backlog estimated are summed up together to
get the total estimated amount of work. This is the starting point on the
burn-down chart. Note that story points are not representative of days or
hours. Each day the number of story points delivered is plotted on a chart to
show the effort remaining burning down. It provides a visual representation
of the work and traceability of the work being completed. As progress is
entered over time you will also start to see the speed at which the team is
performing and get an idea of when the work will be completed. Signs of
any difficulties that may need resolving may be shown on the chart if the
progress starts to slow down or stop.

As you can see from the example in Figure 7.4, the total number of story
points in the product backlog to be delivered is 250 story points. Velocity
has increased slightly over time. In this chart we are measuring the velocity
over iterations. Each iteration could be a two- to four-week time period. The
team have increased their velocity from 10 user story points in the first
iteration to 25 story points. This has stabilized in the last four iterations.
The example burn-down chart in Figure 7.4 shows that the progress line at
its current rate of velocity will reach 0 in iteration 12. This shows when all
the user story points have been delivered and development is complete. In
mature teams user stories are counted instead of story points.

FIGURE 7.4 Burn-down chart

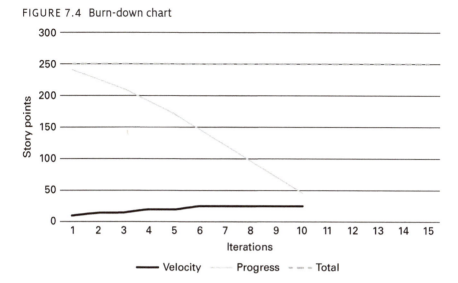

How do you manage changes to requirements?

Managing change in waterfall projects

There must be a process in place to handle changes throughout a project. In a waterfall approach (see Chapter 1 for an explanation) a change process is required as soon as the business requirements have been signed off. A change process will set out all the steps that need to happen to understand the change required, its rationale and the impact it will have as a result. Without this method of control, changes could become impossible to add or could cause scope creep, delaying delivery.

There are four main process steps that need to be agreed and understood. It can be very frustrating if stakeholders think a change is being dealt with and then discover it hasn't been owing to the correct process not being followed or one not existing.

RAISING A CHANGE REQUEST

A change request is a method for raising changes. Decisions need to be made on who can raise a change request, how it is raised and when it is allowed. There may already be a company standard process in place that should be followed. It is worth making sure you understand in advance what this is. It will only be a matter of time before you are asked to be involved with managing a change. If a robust requirements elicitation process is followed there may not be as many change requests but there must be a plan in place to manage changes if and when they do happen.

There is an example of a typical process for raising a change request in the case study on page 186. You will still need to find out what the process is for the company you work at in case it is different. The method to raise a change request will normally be via a change request form, which is a template to ensure the same information is considered in each request for consistency and to ensure the information needed to impact-assess it is provided. It needs to be understood who the recipient of the change request is, and then there will need to be a process for what to do with the change request. There may be occasions when change requests are not allowed during a project, such as during extremely busy periods where there is no time to manage change requests in conjunction with delivery.

The type of information relating to raising a change request will tend to be who you are, what the change is about, why it is needed and when. A change request form is populated in three parts. Raising a change request is the first part of the process.

ASSESSING A CHANGE REQUEST

Once a change request has been raised it will need to be impact-assessed, which is the second part of the process. All the stakeholders responsible for realizing the change request will need to be involved to estimate the amount of work their areas may need to do. There must be an assessment of how to fit the change into the project schedule. If the change is very urgent then there may need to be discussions on whether it impacts existing, signed-off requirements. An assessment will need to take account of the benefits of the change and the risks of not carrying it out, alongside the costs, time impact and impact on other work that needs completing.

There may be more than one option for fulfilling a change request. In these instances, an option paper may be required that lists the options, their pros and cons and a recommendation. If there are likely to be several change requests, a change request log should be created to show all of these in one place for a project. This will help manage and track requests to ensure they are dealt with appropriately and given visibility. A good practice for assessing change requests for large projects is to have a change authority working group who will receive the requests. This will help ensure that multiple perspectives are considered. It will support the change process by reviewing, analysing and facilitating change requests. In addition to this, it will ensure that a proper process, impact assessment and decision making are in place so that any proposed changes can be fully understood and managed.

MAKING A DECISION

Once the request and impact are understood there will need to be a decision on whether to approve the request. This is the third part of the process. During the deciding process the status of the change request should be pending until it can be approved, rejected or deferred. The status should be kept up to date in the change request log.

The decision to approve a change request will depend upon the level of governance. For a low level of governance or a small change with a low expected impact, the project manager may be allowed to approve a change request. For a higher level of governance and on a large project, the decisions may be made as part of the change authority working group described in the previous subsection or as part of the project's steering group. The purpose of a steering group is to provide guidance and strategic direction to the project and to make or ratify the decisions required for the timely delivery of the project deliverables. The composition of the steering group tends to be restricted to the sponsor, project manager and senior stakeholders. However, it is important to understand which of the processes are being followed if you are involved with raising or impact-assessing a change request.

IMPLEMENTING CHANGE REQUESTS

Once a change is approved it will need to be 'planned in' so that work can start on it. Implementing this change will depend upon the priority it has received compared to the other work already being carried out. It may involve updating the business requirements document or solution requirements document, for example. If you get asked to incorporate further changes after a document you have created has been approved, you will need to make the change and update the document to a new version.

Small changes may only require version 1.0 to be updated to 1.1. If there have been many changes or a significant change as a result of the change request, then go up a whole version number to version 2.0. This may require the stakeholders to sign off the document again. To make this process easier, you would first summarize all the changes that have been made to the document as an addendum that can be walked through separately with the stakeholders to keep their focus on the change made. This is to avoid a situation of a stakeholder refusing to sign off based on something separate to the change request.

CASE STUDY

In the Dream Phones case study there were requirements provided about use case UC003 – Conduct phone finder questionnaire (see Chapter 6). In the main flow, the requirements resulted in the customer being given one choice at the end of the questionnaire with an option of requesting a lower or higher budget. These requirements were signed off, but the business realized that there was often more than one phone package that met the customer's criteria, especially if the customer chose more than one brand. The business therefore wanted to raise a change request to select the best of each brand if more than one was chosen.

The information on the change request was filled out by the requestor (Table 7.1).

Once the change request was submitted it was added to the change request log and sent out to the related stakeholders for impact assessment. The second part of the form was filled out by each of the stakeholders and summarized (Table 7.2). As the change request was captured early the impact was quite small.

Once the impact assessment was received the final part of the change request was updated to reflect the decision made (Table 7.3).

TABLE 7.1 Change request

Change request ID	CR00001
Requestor name	Bob Hope
Requestor position	Marketing Manager
Requestor contact details	Bob.hope@Dreamphones.co.uk
Request date	09/09/19
Source of change	Change to solution requirements.
Description of change	If customer has selected more than one brand and the usage details and phone size yield more than one result, then show all relevant options.
Reasons and justification	An investigation into the data and market research has shown that customers regularly want to see more than one brand and there is often more than one brand that matches the customer's usage and phone size criteria.
Priority	Medium.
Rationale for priority	Improved customer experience.

TABLE 7.2 Change request impact assessment

Project management impact assessment	None expected.
Business analysis impact assessment	0.5 days to update documentation and reapproval.
Solution architect impact assessment	No impact as had not started design.
Developer impact assessment	No impact as had not started development.
Tester impact assessment	No impact as had not started testing or building test scripts yet.
Third party supplier impact assessment	No impact.
Please circle the following impacts as a result of the assessments	Schedule cost scope requirements/ deliverables testing/quality resources
Total costs based on impact assessment	Can be absorbed into the current budget at no extra cost.

TABLE 7.3 Change request result

Status – in review, approved, rejected	Approved
Approval date	10/09/19
Approved by	Nigel Lawn

Managing change in agile projects

We have previously covered how agile welcomes changes throughout. Change requests do not get raised. Instead all changes are added to a product backlog. This is the list of all the things the project needs to achieve. Change is instead managed by ordering the items in priority order.

MINIMUM VIABLE PRODUCT (MVP)

The term used for managing the delivery is 'minimum viable product' (MVP). This keeps the focus on implementing small chunks of functionality in order of the items that will provide the greatest amount of value to the customer first. It is important to remember that the focus should be on delivering features in small chunks rather than trying to deliver a whole project at once. This methodology aims to get products to market faster. Therefore, when managing the backlog, the breakdown must be about delivering features that are usable. To understand customer value, techniques such as personas (described in Chapter 3) may be used.

ACHIEVABILITY

Another factor that must be considered is achievability. Only changes that the team believe can be delivered in a time-boxed period can be put forward. This means some changes may be absorbed sooner than others owing to time factors rather than it just being about value.

FEEDBACK

Change may be continual throughout an agile project, because feedback is encouraged when showing the outputs. As feedback is received, changes may be added to make the product better. It can be difficult to get all the details correct first time without having a chance to learn lessons and have continual iterations. If a solution is being put forward that is new to the customer or business, then allowing a continual feedback and iteration process will help improve ideas and achieve a better product.

EXTERNAL ENVIRONMENT

There are some industries and technology advancements where the pace of change is fast. Thus, the speed at which a company can adapt provides a competitive advantage.

08

Enterprise business analysis

Introduction

Enterprise business analysis is important for enabling decision making and managing transformational changes at organizational or departmental level. It is a skill that is becoming much more in demand as businesses realize that many of the business analysis skills that are often applied at project level can also be applied at a more strategic level. Business and technology trends are making the challenges at enterprise level more complex and creating a faster pace of change. This is evidenced by new competitors coming into the market with new business models with lower entrance costs, more sophisticated customers who have a greater access to information, and stronger computing power that can collect and analyse more data to give greater insights.

There are also several business analysis techniques that have been specifically created to work at enterprise level. The chapter will walk you through the business canvas model by means of the fictional case study used throughout this book as an example. Other techniques covered here include SWOT analysis and technology trends. The techniques for understanding the business context and vision covered in Chapter 3 can also contribute to enterprise business analysis. These techniques can all be used to work out strategies and methods for achieving enterprise goals and to identify why and when change is necessary, as well as to provide a foundation for developing hypotheses and ideas.

Finally, the chapter will cover the seven areas that should be considered when assessing an organization's agility. Business agility is the organization's ability to change in response to internal or external factors. Many companies have gone out of business for not recognizing or being able to adapt early enough to change.

Questions answered in this chapter for enterprise business analysis

- What is enterprise business analysis?
- How do you identify new or transformational enterprise initiatives?
- How do you prepare a company for business agility?

What is enterprise business analysis?

Enterprise business analysis is about having a strategic view of the business at an enterprise level. This means being able to apply a business analysis skillset at organizational or departmental level. The benefits of having this strategic view are that it will lead to being able to identify business opportunities, help with making strategic decisions, and enable innovating as well as planning, costing and delivering strategic changes. Interactions at enterprise level are with senior executives and are often done as part of a consultancy role.

Approaches

The main difference with the enterprise business analysis approach is that the enterprise level is focused on value delivered outcomes rather than being task based, which is often the case with projects. It also involves a much greater collaborative effort across the organization. Business architecture or business intelligence teams are regularly set up in some organizations to address the demand in this area. Some organizations train their senior staff using the business analysis skills that are applicable. Another approach could be to set up innovation labs with design thinking initiatives. Design thinking takes a customer-centric approach and looks at how ideas can be generated based on a greater understanding of the customer. Some of these techniques were covered in Chapter 3. The challenges, no matter what approach is taken, are to increase skillsets to tackle more complex business problems and to ensure that the capabilities of the organization are maximized.

How do you identify new or transformational enterprise initiatives?

Business model canvas

A business model canvas can be used to identify the initiatives that an organization should focus on based on nine strategic views. This method involves getting the senior stakeholders together to brainstorm what can be included in each of the nine categories. This is a great technique for start-ups when working to understand each of the different areas and how to achieve them. It can also be useful for enabling major transformation programmes to understand the 'as is' and then to repeat the exercise for the 'to be'. The outputs are not just for the business canvas diagram itself but can also lead to two further planning exercises: one to decide the future initiatives based on the business canvas findings and the other to plan how each of the initiatives will be delivered and when.

There are nine parts.

VALUE PROPOSITIONS

This viewpoint considers the value adding activities available to organizations. It identifies the purposes and the value of what the organization aims to carry out. This may be related to solving customer problems, providing a specialized product or service or identifying what needs the organization is meeting. It is summarized in a couple of words. Sticky notes are ideal for writing on for collating the ideas. Chapter 3 described how to put a customer journey together. This will also help with identifying the value propositions, as it shows what the customer goes through and the emotions. Decisions can then be made on whether value can be added to make the customer happier.

CUSTOMER SEGMENTS

Understanding customers and whether there are different categories for them to fit into is another useful perspective. Looking back at the value propositions will help with identifying the different types of customers and enables questioning on whether the value propositions meet the needs of the customer segments. This will be more straightforward if the business is aiming at niche markets. For mass markets, focus on the types of customer segments that will benefit the most from the value offered. Chapter 3 covered personas, which will also help with identifying the types of customers and their usage of the different value propositions. Segments can be identified in a variety of ways, which could be related to certain industries, job titles, age ranges, spending habits, lifestyles, attitudes and locations, for example. It could be anything that can be used to distinguish between different characteristics, which may then lead to different marketing campaigns or differing needs.

One method for creating distinctions for the mass market is to look at the distinctions that have been made based on the social upbringing of the different generations. Definitions of these age ranges may differ. Listed below are those that are commonly considered, although the relevancy may vary depending upon the country you are from:

- Boomers were born between 1946 and 1964. They have now reached or are reaching retirement, and the sheer volumes of babies born in this generation are generating increased needs in healthcare.

- Generation X were born between 1965 and 1980. This was the first generation in the UK and USA where children were exposed to day care as both parents started to work and where divorce started to become more common. This age group were less concerned with politics or the social issues around them. They tended to have a greater exposure to education. They are technically adept and comfortable with smartphones, email, laptops and other technology.

- Millennials/Generation Y were born between 1981 and 1996. They have increased use of and familiarity with communications, media and digital technologies. They have had great exposure since childhood, so traditional sales techniques are not effective. They want to choose when they buy a product and do their own research.

- Generation Z were born between 1997 and the present. Again, they were or are being brought up in a greater technological age. They are presented as preferring cool products over cool experiences and expect to be able to interact with new technologies in different ways.

These are all generalizations but can be a useful way to understand how to market to the different characteristics.

CHANNELS

Channels determine the communication for reaching the customer segments previously specified and delivering value to the customer. Examples are face to face, by phone, through the internet, via partners, and marketing.

Visualizing the different customer journeys for each of the customer segments can ensure these are captured. You may want to brainstorm current and future possibilities.

CUSTOMER RELATIONSHIPS

Customer relationships address what types of relationships the business has or wants to have with the customers. Relationships may vary for each customer segment. If you are using an 'as is' and 'to be' business canvas model then the differences between them will start to highlight any initiatives required to understand what is needed to bring about changes and how much change is needed.

KEY ACTIVITIES

The key activities for the organization based on the value propositions can be identified by thinking about the activities involved for each value proposition identified. Examples are recruitment, training, marketing and sales.

KEY RESOURCES

This looks at what key resources are needed to support the value propositions. They could be types of people, systems or equipment, for example. Reviewing the key activities will help with thinking about what resources are needed to support each activity.

KEY PARTNERS

The key partners required to support the value propositions are listed. Where key internal resources do not exist, partners are required to deliver some of the activities or to act as suppliers. This therefore helps to identify the relationships required.

REVENUE STREAMS

This sets out the types of revenue streams and pricing strategies.

COST STRUCTURE

The costs involved with creating the value propositions all need to be accounted for. This could include the costs involved with conducting an activity or employing resources. Costs could be fixed, variable, one-off or re-occurring.

CASE STUDY

The management team at the fictional company Dream Phones decide to put together a business canvas model to help them identify the company's future goals (see Figure 8.1). Once they have identified the different contents of the different categories, they will be able to work out what initiatives they want to take forward that support the outcomes of the model.

FIGURE 8.1 Business canvas model

Key partners	Key activities	Value propositions	Customer relationships	Customer segments
Phone suppliers	Sales and marketing	Sell mobile phones	Regularly every time contract due for renewal	Boomers
IT outsourcers	Customer research	Provide advice on phone suitability	Regularly before renewal	Generation X
Shop outfitters	Supplier management	Provide current trends	Ad hoc	Millennials/Generation Y
	Innovation			Generation Z
	Contract management	Provide mobile reviews		
	Purchasing	Provide alerts when renewal due		

Key resources		Channels	
Sales staff	Provide try-out phone	Digital	
Marketing team	experiences in shops	Shops	
Procurement		Phone	
Legal team	Provide phone exchange service	Word of mouth	
Procurement system	Sell phone accessories	Marketing	
Customer database	Changeover service		

Cost structure	Revenue streams
People costs	Commission
Shop outfits	Contract fees
Stock stores	Product sales
Technology provider costs	

SOURCE Strategyzer.com

SWOT analysis

SWOT analysis covers strengths, weaknesses, opportunities and threats. In practice, SWOT is displayed in the format of a grid separated into four quadrants, each with the corresponding heading. When analysing your company or department against each of these categories, SWOT will help drive strategies and enable understanding of what initiatives are required to get there. Strengths and weaknesses are internally focused, whilst opportunities and threats involve an understanding of the wider external environment, such as competitors, the marketplace, trends, technology and customer expectations.

To conduct a SWOT analysis, get a variety of different stakeholders to participate in a workshop. This will ensure different perspectives at different levels. Firstly, set the scene and ensure the vision of the company or department is understood. Ask a senior manager to spend 10–15 minutes providing a summary of the objectives and the vision of what he or she wants to achieve. Separate out the workshop into smaller groups initially with sticky notes and the SWOT grid. Get the attendees to spend five minutes writing down their own thoughts for each category in silence before discussing the results in small groups. Then get one volunteer in each small group to play back their ideas to the whole room and merge them into one big SWOT. This is just one method for how to put a SWOT together. I've suggested this method because it allows for a variety of perspectives. It can then also lead to a brainstorming session on what initiatives are required as a result, which ones need to be strategic and whether there are any quick wins.

Technology trends

EMERGING TECHNOLOGIES

There are technologies that can change and influence how organizations conduct business with their customers and their business models. With technologies such as cloud storage, machine learning, chat bots, big data, 3D printing, expansion of mobile networks to 5G and talking interactions taking more prominence there are many more possibilities for what can be achieved.

Cloud storage makes it far easier to store large volumes of data without being internally restricted to hardware and capacity within the organization. Software services are now offered on a cloud so that organizations can have access faster than ever before to updates without having to do time-intensive installing themselves.

FIGURE 8.2 SWOT grid

Strengths	Weaknesses
Opportunities	Threats

Machine learning is the process by which artificial intelligence software can automate more tasks and make decisions without human intervention and teach itself by analysing patterns of data and behaviour. Google uses machine learning experts extensively. For example, Google has developed an assistant that can make phone calls and understand various nuances in conversations to book hairdressing and restaurant reservations. Another example of machine learning is chat bots making it easier for customers to interact with service providers and making it easier for companies to provide sales and customer care. Customers can go online and interact with a chat bot rather than a human.

With big data, large volumes of data can be analysed quickly and made much more accessible. Queries that previously could take hours to run can now be returned in a fraction of the time.

The technologies of 3D printing are now allowing the printing of inventory just in time. These technologies allow plastics, metals and even human tissue to be printed as and when required, removing the need for large amounts of stock to be stored and changing the way organizations run.

The digital era is expanding communication methods. New generations are growing up with different expectations of how they want to communicate, with far greater access to information. Accessing the internet by means of mobile phone devices will continue to grow as 5G networks are rolled out.

In business analysis it is worth understanding these technologies, because it will help you to understand what questions need to be asked and allows exploration of additional possibilities. This is another reason for making sure the problems are understood and preventing stakeholders jumping straight to solutions. Jumping straight to a solution prevents other options from being assessed.

EXISTING TECHNOLOGIES

In terms of identifying change there may also be a need to review existing systems and technology. An indicator that systems may need replacing is that they are lacking the functionality or quality required. This may be apparent from a heavy reliance on manual processes, sporadic non-integrated systems, out of date and non-supported systems or weak controls.

Other techniques

Techniques for resolving a problem are covered in Chapter 3. This is often a starting point for understanding customers' problems at the enterprise level. Understanding the problem allows innovation because it then opens the door for consideration of several possible solutions. Design thinking provides that customer-centric approach. Process modelling enables an understanding of the 'as is' and 'to be'. Gap analysis can then be conducted to understand what could be improved. Systems thinking allows a holistic view of all the different areas that could be impacting the problem.

How do you prepare a company for business agility?

There are seven major factors that will help prepare an organization for business agility. Business agility is a company's ability to handle changes in response to strategic change, which may be due to external factors or internal transformational changes. The previous section covered techniques for identifying what changes may be required. This section focuses on what needs to be assessed in order to allow the changes to happen.

The seven factors illustrated in Figure 8.3 will now be addressed in turn.

FIGURE 8.3 Factors impacting business agility

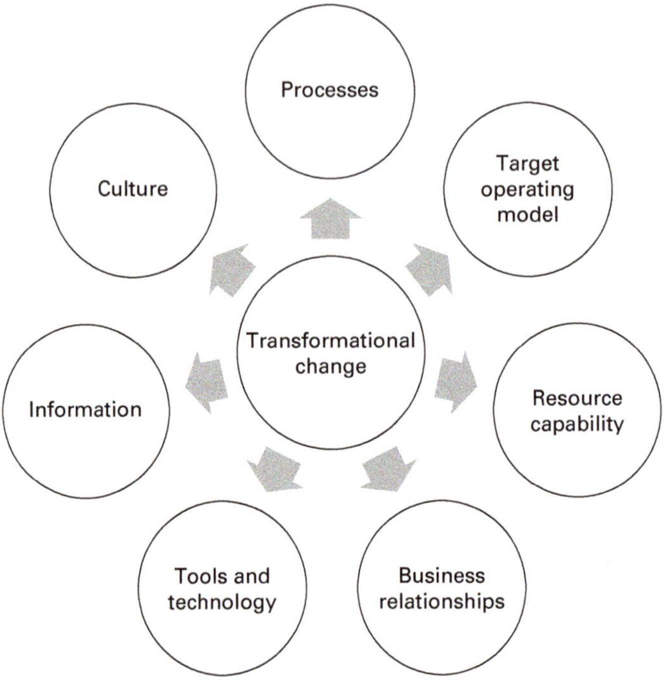

Target operating model

A target operating model sets out how an organization should be structured to support its strategy. It isn't part of the strategy itself, but I've included it under enterprise business analysis because it represents how the business needs to be supported and is at an organizational or departmental level. Target operating models will need to be reviewed to support large process changes, restructures, new businesses or acquisitions and mergers.

Getting the target operating model right is essential in making sure the organization is not only able to meet the strategy but is efficient and keeps pace with the changes required. It involves having an organizational structure with the appropriate hierarchy, job roles, volumes and skillsets to support the company and its processes. It involves the technology supporting the strategy and keeping pace with the changes required within it. It means also planning to have the staff and buildings in the appropriate locations. Once all of these are known, it involves understanding the operating costs and whether the changes being proposed are worth the additional expense or savings.

In terms of engagement you will need good communication and facilitation skills. The only way to understand the 'to be' target operating model is to engage with the senior stakeholders to understand the changes being brought in and how the target operating model needs to change to support them. It may also involve speaking with human resources if there is a risk of employees being displaced. If people are worried about their jobs it is important to act with sensitivity.

If you are asked to get involved with defining a target operating model there is an order that I suggest you follow:

1 principles;

2 assumptions;

3 processes;

4 people;

5 technology;

6 location;

7 operating costs.

PRINCIPLES

It is important to understand any fundamental principles from the outset. These principles will influence decisions to be made and recommendations and should be documented early on and continually revisited.

ASSUMPTIONS

Assumptions must be made when trying to understand what a future target operating model will look like. The future hasn't happened yet so there will be unknowns. Clarifying assumptions makes it easier to understand the figures predicted and will help highlight if any assumptions are not correct. It also helps to ensure all the stakeholders have the same understanding. As and when possible, validate the assumptions. Make sure you state who validated each assumption and when. This will help ensure you know who to go to if any of the assumptions are challenged.

PROCESSES

Processes are the foundation for understanding how many people are required and what technologies are required to support them. Conversations with your stakeholders should be centred around understanding any new processes. You will need to establish if there are any up to date organizational charts that will help you identify the stakeholders. Always start at the top and work down, and ask people who else in their team to engage. Each new process should be analysed to understand what is involved and the volumes expected. It is important to understand all the departments or business areas affected by new or amended processes. All managers whose teams are involved in a process should be engaged to check the impact on their areas. It is good practice to maintain a list of all those engaged so any challenges can be resolved quickly by knowing who to go back to. As the 'to be' target operating model is based on predicting the future there is a high chance that there could be varying opinions in the early stages. This is also why setting out the principles and assumptions is important.

PEOPLE

Once the processes are understood it is easier to assess with each business area manager whether the changes can be absorbed by the existing team structure or whether changes are required as a result of new skillsets or volumes.

For the latter, first define at a high level the changes to staff numbers for each process identified and business area. In addition to volumes you will need to understand the role and the grade. This will provide enough information to identify costs or savings. You may need to liaise with human resources to obtain the expected salary information for the roles and grade. Any further information required will include gaining an understanding of how long any new roles will be required. The managers responsible for their business areas will also help to determine whether full-time permanent employees are required or whether to use day rate or fixed term contractors. If additional people are only required for a short period of time, then the vacancies can be filled with day rate or fixed term contractors and costed accordingly.

The previous information sets out the high level of detail required to explain the number of people needed to support the processes and the costs associated with hiring based on the role, grade and skillset. This information will need to be relayed to senior management to agree the costs or savings made as a result. It is often documented either in spreadsheets or on presentation slides.

TECHNOLOGY

Technology may be required to support changes to the processes. This should also be a consideration when constructing a target operating model.

If there are any changes required to the existing IT systems' architecture, then these will need to be understood and costed. Users of IT systems and IT stakeholders will need to be engaged to find out what currently exists and what changes will be needed. If there are new people required, then this might mean new hardware and software licences to support the onboarding of the new staff. If the changes being made to the business are bigger than this then there will be wider considerations. You will need to establish any changes required to hardware, infrastructure, software, data feeds, maintenance and support, for example. You will need to revisit the principles and assumptions to see whether any more need to be added based on the decisions made around the technology.

LOCATION

This is a consideration if the business is spread over more than one physical location or if the changes to the organization involve changes of location.

OPERATING COSTS

Operating costs are the expenses related to running the business. One of the key criteria when changing a target operating model is understanding the impact to the expenses for the changes made. If a business case is required to make these changes, then a comparison will be required between the operating costs and the financial benefits. Operating costs for changes to people can be obtained by understanding the changes to numbers, and the payroll or expected payroll costs from speaking with the human resources team. Location costs can be ascertained from understanding the costs of new locations or merging of locations. Technology costs can be determined by summing up the changes and costs for the different elements required.

Culture

Culture is the behaviours, beliefs and attitudes of a group of people. A company's culture is central to its ways of working, mindset and capability. To understand what cultural changes are required there will first be a need to understand what the desired culture would look like. In transformation projects there will sometimes be a need to address culture to enable changes to happen. Culture is often the least visible but the most powerful factor for influencing change. If the staff of the company are not fully behind the changes and are not given the support, then there is a strong chance that the transformation will not be as effective. Culture will vary between industries and professions. It will be different for different reasons, and circumstances will vary as to what is the most appropriate.

STEP 1 – IDENTIFICATION

Senior leadership must be engaged to identify and agree on the desired culture along with the reasons for each cultural indicator. There are always two different ends of the spectrum for each indicator, so it is important that the rationale for where the indicator needs to sit on each spectrum is understood and agreed. For example, does the organization value individuals working on their own or is team work more valued? There must be a focus on the behaviours that will make a difference. In an agile project the culture will need to be one of empowerment over hierarchical working, team work over individual work, customer focused over business focused and outcome driven over process driven. These characteristics need to be identified so that action plans can be put together to change the culture if necessary and so they can be measured.

STEP 2 – ENABLEMENT

Once the values required are identified a further analysis is required to understand the 'as is' culture and the size of the gap to move to the 'to be' culture. A popular technique for understanding the 'as is' culture is the use of employee engagement surveys. The feedback from surveys can inform changes that then need to be prioritized to ensure the items supporting the transformation are addressed. To set the scene for enablement, as many people as possible need to be engaged, as it will be this joint effort that enables people to understand the gaps and help take them and others with them on that journey. If people in the organization do not understand the future state vision of the culture and the reasons why, then they will be less likely to help make the changes happen and embed them.

It is important to establish with the leadership team whether there is anything preventing a change in culture. It will also be worth reviewing existing governance, processes, policies, organizational structures, reward schemes, recruitment, technology, renumeration, performance reviews and leadership styles, among other things, to see whether any of these would currently prevent the culture moving to the desired state and which of these need to be changed as part of the action plan.

Putting together an action plan to change the culture can take time and will need a strong communication plan to ensure engagement and an understanding of the changes that need to be made. Not only does the action plan need to apply from the top down, but individuals and teams need to be given the opportunity to help change the culture from the bottom up. This will help instigate buy-in and an understanding of how to help the organization align with the action plan's vision. Working groups could be set up with ownership given to certain members of staff to help make the changes happen. The more people engaged the more likely it is to happen.

STEP 3 – MAINTAINING

Once the action plan is in place there needs to be a drive to ensure it becomes part of everyday life at the company and that the company doesn't revert to the previous culture. Mindsets are hard to change, so a continual drive is required to ensure the new culture is encouraged. The employee survey technique can again be used as a measure for success and to identify any further areas of refinement. Positive behaviours in line with the vision should be rewarded and action taken against negative behaviours.

Resource capability

The capability of resources may also need to be assessed to understand how to move to a 'to be' state or to react to change. A technique to do this involves listing the existing capabilities using a score on a sliding scale from 1 to 5, with 1 indicating no capability, 2 indicating there are significant gaps, 3 indicating that the resource works but could be more effective, 4 indicating that the resource is efficient and effective and 5 indicating that the capability is a competitive advantage. The capabilities and scoring need to be agreed with the management team. The same exercise is repeated for the 'to be' model state. The difference between the scores shows how much change will be required and will allow a plan to be put together to work out how to reduce the gaps.

Business relationships

The type of relationships that organizations have with their key partners and customers will impact how fast they can respond to change. The business canvas model explained earlier in the chapter sets out the types of customer segments and suppliers. An assessment is required as to what the dependencies are on the suppliers and whether there are any risks with lead times or ways of working with the suppliers for implementing changes. The relationship with customers can also be valuable. Identify whether any groups can be used for market research and for obtaining feedback. Being able to get early feedback will help ensure changes impacting customers are assessed early enough to make further adaptations if necessary, to obtain a competitive advantage. Design thinking techniques such as those described in Chapter 3 can also be used to get a better understanding of the customer.

Tools and technology

STRATEGY

Agility in technology terms will involve a company having a clear IT strategy that supports and underpins the wider business strategy. An understanding of what is termed 'disruptive technologies', such as cloud technology, big data and machine learning, opens new possibilities.

A review of existing technologies will ascertain how well they are supporting the business strategy. If the IT department are not aware of all their applications being used, there are more risks that the technologies are not supporting the business strategy. This tends to happen when there is a lack of system capabilities and reporting and the business attempts to plug the gaps by producing end user applications itself. It might be a suitable short-term measure to support the business but then increases risks of excessive manual processes, outdated non-supported systems and a lack of integration with other systems. The impact to the business is a reliance on its people for specialized knowledge of the system, higher costs and generally a fire-fighting approach.

GOVERNANCE AND CONTROLS

Visibility of all the IT systems is needed, along with strong controls and governance. Controls should be proactive and preventative, not reactive and detective.

IT INFRASTRUCTURE

Systems will need to be integrated where appropriate.

DATA STRATEGY AND REPORTING

Data should be reliable and valid. There should be a clear data strategy that maps from the source to the report. This will impact business agility if there is a reliance on data to enable the making of decisions or if there are lots of manual processes created to check and validate data.

SCALABILITY

An assessment is required of how scalable the systems are to support the business strategy and of the projected growth changes that will be needed to support strategic change.

SUPPORTED AND FUTURE-PROOFED SYSTEMS

If there are lots of unsupported and tactical systems that are impacted by the changes that need to be made, it will make the work required more difficult. More time will need to be spent on working out what to do with these systems and whether they need to be replaced by more strategic solutions. This will therefore have a knock-on impact on how quickly a business can respond to change.

Information

Accessibility to information will aid decision making. How easy it is to obtain information will impact an organization's ability to respond to change. An assessment may be required of what information is needed to make management decisions and how accessible and reliable it is.

Processes

An organization's processes will have a big impact on how easily the organization can respond to change. If the processes are very manually intensive or not documented or visible, then preparing for changes will be more difficult. See Chapter 4 for more details on how to conduct process modelling and its benefits.

09

Templates

Introduction

Templates set out a basic structure of what a document should contain and a consistent look and feel. The previous chapters have detailed approaches, questions to ask and techniques. This chapter will explain some of the types of templates you will find useful. These will save time and avoid having to create a document from scratch each time. Your company may already have standardized templates. If it hasn't then the templates here will be a good starting point.

The chapter includes some best practice guidelines that need to be part of any template. This will be useful if you are having to create your own templates, update existing templates or create your own document from scratch. There are also tips for managing expectations whilst in the process of producing the documentation and how to reflect to stakeholders the difference between a signed-off document and one where their input is still required.

See Figure 9.1 for a recap on some of the documentation covered previously and the related templates covered in this chapter.

Questions answered in this chapter about templates

- What are the best practice guidelines when documenting?
- What are the benefits and drawbacks of having templates?
- What does a template look like for a vision document?
- What does a template look like for a business process document?
- What does a template look like for a business requirements document?
- What does a template look like for a solution requirements document?

FIGURE 9.1 Summary overview of templates

Chapter	Chapter 3 Business context and vision	Chapter 4 Business context and business processes	Chapter 5 Business context/understanding requirements	Chapter 6 System context/understanding requirements
Summary	Business context is about the current situation and environment. The vision is about understanding what the business wants to achieve and how its success can be measured. These concepts set out the direction of change.	Process modelling is a way to show visually what happens in an organization or department, or the route to achieving a goal to ensure a common understanding, allow analysis and identify improvements.	Business requirements are written from the point of view of the stakeholders, focusing on what they want in relation to the objectives specified in the vision.	This lower level of detail sets out how the solution needs to function and behave in order to meet the business requirements.
Related documentation	 Vision document	 Business process document	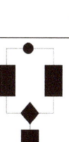 Business requirements document	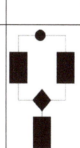 Solution requirements document

What are the best practice guidelines when documenting?

There are standard guidelines for most types of documentation relating to business analysis. Each one will tend to have the following components:

- title page – containing title, author, version number and location where the document is stored;
- contents page – a list of the contents in the document;
- glossary – to explain any acronyms or business terms;
- executive summary – a brief summary as to the contents of the document;
- purpose of document – to explain what the document sets out to achieve;
- reference numbers – each heading, paragraph and requirement should have a reference associated with it;
- log – a log of all of the assumptions, risks, issues, decisions and dependencies relating to the documentation;
- document control page – sets out a revision history of all versions distributed and the changes made, the names and roles of the reviewers, and the names and dates of sign-off from the approvers.

It is good practice to use watermarks to show when your document is still a draft. This makes it clear to the audience it is a draft and changes are still allowed to it to obtain their feedback. Another indicator that the document is a draft is that the version number on the front cover is less than 1. However, having a watermark saying 'draft' on each page makes it much clearer to the readers no matter what page they are on.

Further good practice is to ensure you get your documents peer-reviewed. This is because it can be too easy to make assumptions without realizing it. Having someone who isn't as close to the project as you review it will help to identify how to clarify any assumptions made and will make sure anyone new picking up the document still understands its contents.

Once the document is ready for the stakeholders to review, their feedback must be obtained and incorporated if necessary. Refer to Chapter 7 if you want more detail about obtaining feedback for documentation.

What are the benefits and drawbacks of having templates?

Benefits

Templates help provide consistency across all documentation and over time. A template sets out the basic structure and headings expected in it. It also can provide corporate branding. It ensures the same headings are used, with consideration given to each. This makes sure less experienced team members know what is expected of them and helps to bring documentation up to a higher standard. It enables new techniques to be embedded and development areas to be recognized. Another benefit is that the templates can be used to promote to teams outside the business analysis team to educate stakeholders on the quality of documentation expected and the type of information needed for each. This will help with collaboration and understanding of the business analysis role.

Drawbacks

Despite the benefits, there can be drawbacks if the templates are seen as over-engineered for some projects or if they are hard to understand. Templates should be refined over time to meet the needs of the business. Someone should always be nominated to own a template of a document so if there are changes required it can be updated relatively easily. Training may be required to ensure each person responsible for creating the document has the necessary skills to populate it.

Vision document template

This is a template. Writing in italics is for guidance only. Please remove before distributing document. This is the cover sheet. You can also add the company logo on this page.

Project name:

Version:

Date:

Author:

File location:

Sponsor:

Contents

1. Executive summary

1.1. Purpose of document

The purpose of a vision document is:

- to understand the objectives of the changes required and the business needs;
- to ensure the change will resolve the right problem and not move the problem elsewhere;
- to understand the success criteria, dependencies and constraints that would impact possible solutions;
- to identify a list of potential options for implementing the changes and provide a recommended approach;
- to enable an impact assessment to understand the size and complexity of the work and the priority.

1.2. Introduction

No more than a couple of paragraphs to set the context.

1.3. Project objectives

1.3.1. IN SCOPE
Set out the objectives.

1.3.2. OUT OF SCOPE
Need to explain why areas have been called out of scope so it is clear what the decisions were around this.

1.4. Associated documents

Document name	Version	Location
		<insert hyperlink>
		<insert hyperlink>
		<insert hyperlink>

1.5. *Glossary*

Term	Meaning

---

2. Problem statement

Success criteria should consider any constraints such as resources, methodology, solution/ technology, contracts, company policy, governance and physical. Be careful with these, as they could discount solutions that would otherwise resolve the problems specified.

2.1. *The problems and why*

2.2. *Who is affected and when*

2.3. *The impact of the problems*

2.4. *Success criteria required of a solution*

3. Work context

3.1. *Context diagram*

Add context diagram here, followed by a description of each team or external interface identified. Include numbers in a team, how often they will use the change under consideration and when.

4. Summary of needs

4.1. *Regulation*

Any regulatory impacts need to be summarized. This makes it clear what is compulsory and requires a solution. For example, it could be changes to company policy, authorization, principles, new rules, treating customers fairly, record keeping and many others.

Name	Description of any regulations impacted	Why impacted?	Priority

4.2. Controls

An understanding is required of what controls must be in place. This could relate to communication, staff, procedures, decisions or controls around processes or calculations, for instance.

Name	Description of controls impacted	Why impacted?	Priority

4.3. Business processes

It is useful to understand the business processes impacted. This will help ascertain the size of the project. The number of processes will also be a good indicator to the size and complexity of the project.

Name	Description of processes impacted	Why impacted?	Priority

4.4. Communications with customer

Communications such as letters and documents are a useful indicator as to the size of a project. If at this stage the number is not known, then assumptions can be stated for future validation and the types of changes can be listed.

Name	Description of customer communication impacted	Why impacted?	Priority

4.5. Management information and reporting

This is to bring out whether the solution needs to incorporate any management information (MI) or reporting. At a high level it should state what type of reports are needed and for whom.

Name	Description of MI and reporting impacted	Why impacted?	Priority

4.6. Organizational structure

Any organizational changes need to be specified. For example, if there are new processes then there may need to be additional skills not currently available.

Name	Description of any parts of the organizational structure impacted	Why impacted?	Priority

4.7. Data

To confirm whether there are any changes required to existing data or any new data not currently collected or stored.

Name	Description of data impacted	Why impacted?	Priority

4.8. Strategic planning

To state whether any strategic planning is required and whether any solution must be in line with the strategic business direction.

Name	Description of strategic planning impacted	Why impacted?	Priority

4.9. Our offering impact

To identify how our offering to customers or third parties is impacted. This could be related to services or products.

Name	Description of our offering impacted	Why impacted?	Priority

4.10. Learning and development

Is it envisaged that any new training materials will be required or whether any training needs will be rolled out?

Name	Description of learning and development impacted	Why impacted?	Priority

4.11. Timelines

State any timelines that need to be met and the importance of meeting deadlines, including why.

Name	Description of timelines impacted	Why impacted?	Priority

5. Solutions evaluated

5.1. Introduction

Set out the approach for the solutions evaluated.

5.2. Option 1

5.2.1. DESCRIPTION OF OPTION

5.2.2. PROS

5.2.3. CONS

5.3. Option 2

5.3.1. DESCRIPTION OF OPTION

5.3.2. PROS

5.3.3. CONS

5.4. Option 3

5.4.1. DESCRIPTION OF OPTION

5.4.2. PROS

5.4.3. CONS

5.5. Recommended option

Explain which option was chosen and the reasons why.

5.6. Summary of costs

State who will be required to make the change happen. How many days' effort will be required from each, and have their day rates been calculated? Hardware and software costs will need to be collated, including any consultancy and licence costs.

5.6.1. DEVELOPMENT COSTS

5.6.2. RUNNING COSTS

6. Log

This log should appear in most of the business analysis documentation. It sets out the decisions, assumptions, issues, risks and dependencies that might impact the document. They should then be reflected in the project's central log.

6.1. Decisions

The following decisions have been identified:

Ref	Decision	Who made	When

6.2. Assumptions

The following assumptions have been identified:

Ref	Assumption	When	Date validated	Validated by

6.3. Issues

The following issues have been identified:

Ref	Issue	Date raised	Raised by	When

6.4. Risks

The following risks have been identified:

Ref	Risk	Mitigation	Raised by	When

6.5. Dependencies

The following dependencies have been identified:

Ref	Dependency	Raised by	When

7. Document control

This should appear in most of the business analysis documentation. It sets out the revision history of the document, who needs to review or require it for information purposes and who needs to sign it off to show its contents have been agreed.

7.1. Revision history

Each time the document is distributed it should be updated with a new version number. This is to ensure all of the stakeholders are looking at the correct version and they have a summary of what has changed since they last received it. The first version is normally 0.1 and labelled as first draft. Each subsequent version should go up by 0.1 each time. When it is signed off it can be updated to version 1.

This document has had the following revisions:

Revision date	Version	Summary of changes	Author	Signed off by	Signed off date

7.2. Review/distribution

This document has been distributed to the following for review/information:

Name	Role	Date issued	Reviewer or for information	Version no.

7.3. Needs sign-off

The needs can be signed off once sections 1, 2, 3 and 4 are complete. The needs should be signed off before identifying the possible solutions in section 5.

By approving this document, you are confirming it complies with the documentation standards, feedback on any issues/discrepancies has been provided, and these have been adequately addressed.

Name and role or forum	Date	Supporting evidence (email/ meeting minutes)

7.4. Options sign-off

The options are to be signed off once section 5 is complete after the needs have been approved.

By approving this document, you are confirming it complies with the documentation standards, feedback on any issues/discrepancies has been provided, and these have been adequately addressed.

Name and role or forum	Date	Supporting evidence (email/ meeting minutes)

Business process document template

This is a template. Writing in italics is for guidance only. Please remove before distributing document. This is the cover sheet. You can also add the company logo on this page.

Project name:

Version:

Date:

Author:

File location:

Contents

1. Executive summary

1.1. Purpose

This sets out the business's 'as is' and 'to be' processes to understand the activities of the business prior to a change and what the desired activities would be after a change. The 'as is' state can be analysed to identify problems and opportunities for change. It also provides an understanding of the processes end to end, as if a process goes across teams then the different teams may only know their part in the process. It is only by looking at the complete picture that analysis can be conducted on what improvements can be made. This artefact should always be documented and agreed prior to the business requirements document. This is because it helps towards understanding the scope of the requirements and all business requirements should relate to a process.

1.2. Introduction

No more than a couple of paragraphs to set the context.

1.3. Project objectives

1.3.1. IN SCOPE
Sets out the business processes that are in scope.

1.3.2. OUT OF SCOPE
Sets out the business processes that are not in scope. You will need to explain why areas have been called out of scope, as this logic may be challenged as the project proceeds.

1.4. Opportunities

State here the opportunities to be realized.

1.5. Associated documents

Document name	Version	Location
		<insert hyperlink>
		<insert hyperlink>
		<insert hyperlink>

2. End to end high-level business processes

2.1. Triggers/business events

This is to identify the business events for each process diagram required. These can also be described as goals. Examples are: 'I want to buy a book', 'I want to pay the credit card at the end of the month', etc.

A trigger is what starts the business event. It may be a person, a system or time.

Trigger	Business event/goal

2.2. 'As is' business processes

Add a business process diagram to this section. A decision must be made as to whether to understand the 'as is' process or go straight to the 'to be' process. The 'as is' is useful for understanding where the pain points are and how the process can be improved.

2.3. 'To be' business processes

Add a business process diagram to this section. The 'to be' process will allow an understanding of what requirements are to be in scope for the project and ensures that the requirements do not duplicate problems relating to old, inefficient processes.

3. Log

This log should appear in most of the business analysis documentation. It sets out the decisions, assumptions, issues, risks and dependencies that might impact the document. They should then be reflected in the project's central log.

3.1. Decisions

The following decisions have been identified:

Ref	Decision	Who made	When

3.2. Assumptions

The following assumptions have been identified:

Ref	Assumption	When	Date validated	Validated by

3.3. Issues

The following issues have been identified:

Ref	Issue	Date raised	Raised by	When

3.4. Risks

The following risks have been identified:

Ref	Risk	Mitigation	Raised by	When

3.5. Dependencies

The following dependencies have been identified:

Ref	Dependency	Raised by	When

4. Appendix A – process key

FIGURE 9.2 BPMN symbols

Symbol	Name	Description
Events		
Start	Start event	Symbolizes the start of a process. You can add the word 'start' or what the trigger is as a narrative or leave it blank.
End	End event	Shows the end of the process. You can add the word 'end' or the result of the process or leave it blank. There could be more than one end event in a process if there is more than one outcome.
Participants		
Company A / Sales / IT	Pool and swim lanes	A pool is represented by Company A in the illustration example. It should always accompany one or more swim lanes. It will generally be used to represent different boundaries such as company level in a process or swim lanes belonging in different boundaries. A swim lane shows the different participants typically being used to show activities carried out by different departments or roles.
Activities		
	Activity	Represents each activity carried out as part of a process. The naming convention for activities should be short and consist of a verb and an object.
⊞	Collapsed sub-process	If you wish to show that an activity has been broken down further in a separate process diagram, then the plus symbol can be used.
Connecting objects		
⟶	Sequence flow	Shows sequence and helps in navigating through the process and knowing what order to follow.
○- - - - - -▷	Message flow	The sequence flow is not used when showing the relationship between two tasks in different pools. Instead the message flow symbol is used.
Gateways		
◇	XOR gateway	Represents a decision or more than one option that applies before proceeding to the next task. A question is often asked in conjunction with this symbol being used, and it will have a minimum of two sequence flows going out of it with the different options possible.
Data		
	Data store with association symbol	This can be used to show which tasks use a system or have data stored centrally. The association symbol represented by the dotted line attaches to the relevant tasks. The data store can be named to show the system that the stakeholders are familiar with.
	Data object	This can be used to show which tasks can be associated with different types of documentation. It could be a report, form, guide etc. The association symbol represented by the dotted line attaches to the relevant tasks. The data object can be named with the documentation that the stakeholders are familiar with.

FIGURE 9.3 Additional BPMN symbols

Symbol	Name	Description
 	Activity with a throwing or receiving message event symbol	The shaded envelope represents a send communication. The unshaded envelope represents a receive communication. They come as a pair. Wherever you have a send message you will have a corresponding receive one. These are normally used when activities go from one swim lane to another to show the handoffs.
	Activity that shows a user using a system	A little person symbol shows which activities involve a user using a system to complete it.
	Activity that is automated by software	Two little cogs represent an automated system activity.
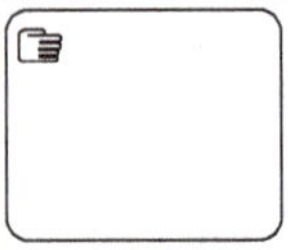	Activity that is manual and carried out by a human	A little hand symbol represents manual activities.

5. Document control

This should appear in most of the business analysis documentation. It sets out the revision history of the document, who needs to review or require it for information purposes and who needs to sign it off to show its contents have been agreed.

5.1. Revision history

Each time the document is distributed it should be updated with a new version number. This is to ensure all of the stakeholders are looking at the correct version and they have a summary of what has changed since they last received it. The first version is normally 0.1 and labelled as first draft. Each subsequent version should go up by 0.1 each time. When it is signed off it can be updated to version 1.

This document has had the following revisions:

Revision date	Version	Summary of changes	Author	Signed off by	Signed off date

5.2. Review/distribution

This document has been distributed to the following for review/information:

Version no.	Name	Role	Date issued	Reviewer or for information

5.3. Sign-off

By approving this document, you are confirming it complies with the documentation standards, feedback on any issues/discrepancies has been provided, and these have been adequately addressed.

Name and role or forum	Date	Supporting evidence (email/ meeting minutes)

Business requirements document template

This is a template. Writing in italics is for guidance only. Please remove before distributing document. This is the cover sheet. You can also add the company logo on this page.

Project name:

Version:

Date:

Author:

File location:

Contents

1. Executive summary

1.1. Purpose of document

The purpose of a business requirements document is to set out what is required. It should not contain solutions. This document enables the business to make sure a common understanding has been obtained before proceeding with a solution. It also acts as a checklist to ensure success can be measured and to enable testing back to what was identified.

1.2. Introduction

No more than a couple of paragraphs to set the context.

1.3. Project objectives

1.4. In scope

This should be in line with the objectives agreed for this project.

1.5. Out of scope

Need to explain why areas have been called out of scope, as this logic may be challenged as the project proceeds.

1.6. Associated documents

Document name	Version	Location
		\<insert hyperlink\>
		\<insert hyperlink\>
		\<insert hyperlink\>

1.7. *Glossary*

Term	Meaning

2. Work context

2.1. *Table*

The work context defines the boundaries for the requirements. This shows what the project is responsible for and what is the responsibility of others outside of the project.

An actor may be a person or a system that interacts externally to the work context.

Identify all of the inputs and outputs, including what business areas and systems need to input into the work context or what outputs they need to receive.

Questions for identifying inputs and outputs include:

- *What forms do you use?*
- *What types of information are going into the work context?*
- *What outputs are received?*
- *What reports are received?*

This provides an opportunity for you to get copies of any forms or reports that are fed into or should come out of the system. Remember always to ask how up to date and complete these are.

The inputs and outputs or the 'to be' process tasks identified as being in scope can be used to establish the use cases. The use cases set out the scope of the work by establishing all of the types of things that need to be carried out. These can then be estimated separately or used to group the requirements.

Actor	Use case	Inputs	Outputs
Customer services	Perform customer verification	Loan quote requested	Customer verified

2.2. Use case model

Add the use case model.

3. Business requirements

State here all the business/stakeholder requirements using the use cases identified as a guide for grouping.

3.1. Detailed requirements

Ref	Business use case	Description	Priority	Source	Rationale

3.2. Requirements prioritization summary

3.2.1. TARGET

The table overleaf shows the maximum percentages allowed for the requirements given.

Priority	Definition	Maximum requirement %
Very high	Very high value to the business and no manual workarounds available. The project cannot be a success without this.	20
High	High value to the business and only limited or costly manual workarounds available. The project benefits would be significantly impacted if this requirement isn't met.	40
Medium	Medium value to the business. Manual workarounds are available, but the benefits to the project will not be as significantly impacted.	20
Low	Low value to the business. This is nice to have if time and cost allow it. Benefits to the project can still be delivered.	20
Total		100 %

3.2.2. ACTUALS SUMMARY

The table below shows the actual requirement allocation.

Priority	Number of requirements	Number of requirements %
Very high		
High		
Medium		
Low		
Total		

4. Business domain model

Creation of a business domain model can flush out missing requirements, especially for regulatory/data heavy projects.

A class or entity is a group of data with connected characteristics. The different characteristics are known as attributes.

4.1. Business domain model diagram

Enter diagram here.

4.2. Data dictionary

4.2.1. <ENTITY 1>

Replace <Entity 1> with the title of each of the entities in the diagram and repeat the subheading and table for each.

Description: *Add a description of the entity.*

Attribute name	Description	
		Mandatory/optional
		Type
		Length
		Format
		Validation
		Default
		Example
		Mandatory/optional
		Type
		Length
		Format
		Validation
		Default
		Example
		Mandatory/optional
		Type
		Length
		Format
		Validation
		Default
		Example
		Mandatory/optional
		Type
		Length
		Format
		Validation
		Default
		Example

5. Log

This log should appear in most of the business analysis documentation. It sets out the decisions, assumptions, issues, risks and dependencies that might impact the document. They should then be reflected in the project's central log.

5.1. Decisions

The following decisions have been identified:

Ref	Decision	Who made	When

5.2. Assumptions

The following assumptions have been identified:

Ref	Assumption	When	Date validated	Validated by

5.3. Issues

The following issues have been identified:

Ref	Issue	Date raised	Raised by	When

5.4. Risks

The following risks have been identified:

Ref	Risk	Mitigation	Raised by	When

5.5. Dependencies

The following dependencies have been identified:

Ref	Dependency	Raised by	When

6. Document control

This should appear in most of the business analysis documentation. It sets out the revision history of the document, who needs to review or require it for information purposes and who needs to sign it off to show its contents have been agreed.

6.1. Revision history

Each time the document is distributed it should be updated with a new version number. This is to ensure all of the stakeholders are looking at the correct version and they have a summary of what has changed since they last received it. The first version is normally 0.1 and labelled as first draft. Each subsequent version should go up by 0.1 each time. When it is signed off it can be updated to version 1.

This document has had the following revisions:

Revision date	Version	Summary of changes	Author	Signed off by	Signed off date

6.2. *Review/distribution*

This document has been distributed to the following for review/information:

Name	Role	Date issued	Reviewer or for information	Version no.

6.3. *Sign-off*

By approving this document, you are confirming it complies with the documentation standards, feedback on any issues/discrepancies has been provided, and these have been adequately addressed.

Name and role or forum	Date	Supporting evidence (email/ meeting minutes)

Solution requirements document template (UML)

This is a template. Writing in italics is for guidance only. Please remove before distributing document. This is the cover sheet. You can also add the company logo on this page.

Project name:

Use case name:

Version:

Date:

Author:

File location:

Contents

1. Purpose of document

The purpose of a use case model document is to set out the system requirements for a use case to ensure it is understood and acceptable to the business and IT stakeholders. It sets out how the stakeholder requirements are going to be met.

2. Use case name

Replace title with the name of the use case being explored.

2.1. Description

One or two sentences to describe the use case.

2.2. Priority

An understanding can be specified here on the importance of the use case. Would the system be worth developing without it?

2.3. Justification

This is to explain why the use case is needed and to supplement the priority given.

2.4. Pre-conditions

This is the state of the system before the use case.

2.5. Post-conditions

This is the state of the system after the use case.

2.6. Basic path

This details the main scenario that occurs in sequence order.

Main success scenario	1
	2
	3
	4
	5
	6
	7
	8
	9

2.7. Alternative path – this alternative path occurs when...

Repeat this subsection for each alternative path, populating the rest of the heading with what causes this alternative flow. The step numbering should reflect where it branches off from the main flow, using an additional letter in alphabetical order for each alternative, followed by a sequence number.

Alternative scenarios	2a1
	2a2
	2a3

2.8. Special requirements

This contains any non-functional requirements specific to the use case or business rules to be adhered to. This isn't a mandatory section and is only populated when applicable.

3. Log

This log should appear in most of the business analysis documentation. It sets out the decisions, assumptions, issues, risks and dependencies that might impact the document. They should then be reflected in the project's central log.

3.1. Decisions

The following decisions have been identified:

Ref	Decision	Who made	When

3.2. *Assumptions*

The following assumptions have been identified:

Ref	Assumption	When	Date validated	Validated by

3.3. *Issues*

The following issues have been identified:

Ref	Issue	Date raised	Raised by	When

3.4. *Risks*

The following risks have been identified:

Ref	Risk	Mitigation	Raised by	When

3.5. *Dependencies*

The following dependencies have been identified:

Ref	Dependency	Raised by	When

4. Document control

This should appear in most of the business analysis documentation. It sets out the revision history of the document, who needs to review or require it for information purposes and who needs to sign it off to show its contents have been agreed.

4.1. Revision history

Each time the document is distributed it should be updated with a new version number. This is to ensure all of the stakeholders are looking at the correct version and they have a summary of what has changed since they last received it. The first version is normally 0.1 and labelled as first draft. Each subsequent version should go up by 0.1 each time. When it is signed off it can be updated to version 1.

This document has had the following revisions:

Revision date	Version	Summary of changes	Author	Signed off by	Signed off date

4.2. Review/distribution

This document has been distributed to the following for review/information:

Name	Role	Date issued	Reviewer or for information	Version no.

4.3. *Use case sign-off*

By approving this document, you are confirming it complies with the documentation standards, feedback on any issues/discrepancies has been provided, and these have been adequately addressed.

Name and role or forum	Date	Supporting evidence (email/ meeting minutes)

AGILE TEMPLATE
This template should be repeated for each story.

Level (theme, epic, user story):

Title:

Approved by product owner (Y/N):

Owner assigned:

Labels:

Priority:

Estimated story points:

Due date:

Release:

Sprint:

Description:

Acceptance criteria:

Attachments:

Tasks:

Issues:

Solution requirements document template (non-functional)

This is a template. Writing in italics is for guidance only. Please remove before distributing document. This is the cover sheet. You can also add the company logo on this page.

Project name:

Version:

Date:

Author:

File location:

Contents

1. Introduction

1.1. Purpose

The purpose of this document is to define the non-functional requirements. This is to enable IT to design a solution suitable from both a technical and a business perspective relating to the quality of it rather than what it functionally has to do.

1.2. Related documentation

Document name	Version	Location
		<insert hyperlink>
		<insert hyperlink>
		<insert hyperlink>

1.3. Glossary

Term	Meaning

2. Non-functional requirements

2.1. Implementation requirements

To include constraints and expectations around implementation. This may be due to the existing company infrastructure. These requirements will most likely be from the enterprise or solution architects, as they will be most familiar with the IT landscape and what is possible. It could include web browser versions and other software that needs to be supported. It could also include hardware and networking requirements.

2.2. Support requirements

To set out what is required to support the new solution. This could be due to an incident, change management, service levels and escalation management. The IT support manager should be engaged to establish the current support available. Then architects and the business will need to agree whether there are any gaps as a result of the new solution and the feasibility for any changes.

2.3. Back-up and recovery requirements

To set out what needs to be backed up to prevent a loss of data or system functionality as a result of an incident and the frequency. Also to define time limits for getting the data back based on business importance. To be obtained from the business and IT stakeholders from the point of view of the business and the feasibility from an IT perspective.

2.4. Performance requirements

Includes how fast the system needs to perform. This could be in terms of response times, processing times or query and reporting times. Sourced from understanding end user expectations, investigating existing levels of performance or finding out industry standards.

2.5. Availability requirements

To define when the system needs to be available and its locations. Again, a mixture of business and IT stakeholders will need to be consulted. Analysis required of when the business needs the system to be available and what availability the IT department currently support and the gaps.

2.6. Capacity requirements

To set out what current and future volumes the system needs to support and the number of users and concurrent users required. Business stakeholders might be able to provide assistance with this or an analysis of the current types of data impacted by the system.

2.7. Security requirements

To ensure security of the systems and the data involved. Sourced from IT security, business stakeholders and security policy documentation. Takes into consideration user access, roles, authentication, how data are stored, encryption and infrastructure.

2.8. Archiving requirements

To set out what needs to be archived, when, how retrieved and when deleted. Requirements can be established from asking the business stakeholders how long they will need to use the data for and by speaking to data governance and compliance to find out the policies on data retention.

2.9. Auditability requirements

To set out requirements on what data need to be tracked in terms of who changes data, when and what changes were made. These requirements can be sourced from business or IT stakeholders who may need to investigate the reasons for a change. There could also be standard security or IT standards that could impact this.

2.10. Usability requirements

To set out any requirements related to look and feel, user skill levels, error messages and help facilities. Sources for this information may be from using the business stakeholders' knowledge of the users, user research and existing branding guidelines or creative designs.

3. Log

This log should appear in most of the business analysis documentation. It sets out the decisions, assumptions, issues, risks and dependencies that might impact the document. They should then be reflected in the project's central log.

3.1. Decisions

The following decisions have been identified:

Ref	Decision	Who made	When

3.2. Assumptions

The following assumptions have been identified:

Ref	Assumption	When	Date validated	Validated by

3.3. *Issues*

The following issues have been identified:

Ref	Issue	Date raised	Raised by	When

3.4. *Risks*

The following risks have been identified:

Ref	Risk	Mitigation	Raised by	When

3.5. *Dependencies*

The following dependencies have been identified:

Ref	Dependency	Raised by	When

4. Document control

This should appear in most of the business analysis documentation. It sets out the revision history of the document, who needs to review or require it for information purposes and who needs to sign it off to show its contents have been agreed.

4.1. *Revision history*

Each time the document is distributed it should be updated with a new version number. This is to ensure all of the stakeholders are looking at the correct version and they have a

summary of what has changed since they last received it. The first version is normally 0.1
and labelled as first draft. Each subsequent version should go up by 0.1 each time. When
it is signed off it can be updated to version 1.

This document has had the following revisions:

Revision date	Version	Summary of changes	Author	Signed off by	Signed off date

4.2. Review/distribution

This document has been distributed to the following for review/information:

Name	Role	Date issued	Reviewer or for information	Version no.

4.3. Sign-off

By approving this document, you are confirming it complies with the documentation
standards, feedback on any issues/discrepancies has been provided, and these have
been adequately addressed.

Name and role or forum	Date	Supporting evidence (email/ meeting minutes)

Solutions requirements document template (business solutions)

This is a template. Writing in italics is for guidance only. Please remove before distributing document. This is the cover sheet. You can also add the company logo on this page.

Project name:

Version:

Date:

Author:

Business area:

File location:

Contents

1. Introduction

1.1. Purpose

The purpose of a business solutions document is:

- to set out the proposed business solutions for <project name>;
- to build upon the impact assessment with the business and identify what it needs to put in place for business readiness.

2. Business requirements

2.1. Summary

Add a summary of the business requirements that require a business solution.

3. Scope

3.1. In scope

Set out the scope being covered, for example new or changed services being offered, new support models, processes, procedures, recruitment, resources, training etc.

3.2. Out of scope

Set out what isn't being covered.

4. Business problem statement

4.1. Problem to resolve

Set out the problems that will be resolved by this business solutions document. Set out each problem identified under a new reference number.

4.2. A successful solution will...

Set out the criteria for success. This will relate back to the problems and how they are resolved.

5. Solution proposed

Each subheading to relate to each of the different business solutions, with more detail provided underneath. Only include the subheadings required or add new ones where applicable. For example, subheadings could be based on new roles, new processes etc. The detail could describe what is required or show business process model diagrams.

5.1. Organizational structure changes

This section is required if there are any changes required to the headcount. Include details on any new roles required, responsibilities and funding.

5.2. Business process changes

This section is required if there are new business processes to be communicated or agreed.

5.3. Meeting changes

This section is required if there are any additional meetings and communication required. Set out each new meeting if needed, along with the purpose of it, the attendees and the objectives.

5.4. Documentation changes

This section is required if there is any new documentation required. It should then set out under a separate subheading for each document its purpose, who creates and updates it, who can access it and when it is used.

5.5. Workflow changes

This section is required to agree any changes to workflow.

6. Costs

Add any costs associated with the changes, for example recruitment. If there is more than one option, then the different options can be provided along with a recommended option.

7. Log

This log should appear in most of the business analysis documentation. It sets out the decisions, assumptions, issues, risks and dependencies that might impact the document. They should then be reflected in the project's central log.

7.1. Decisions

The following decisions have been identified:

Ref	Decision	Who made	When

7.2. Assumptions

The following assumptions have been identified:

Ref	Assumption	When	Date validated	Validated by

7.3. Issues

The following issues have been identified:

Ref	Issue	Date raised	Raised by	When

7.4. Risks

The following risks have been identified:

Ref	Risk	Mitigation	Raised by	When

7.5. Dependencies

The following dependencies have been identified:

Ref	Dependency	Raised by	When

8. Appendix A – role profiles

An appendix can be added to provide any levels of detail that are useful but do not belong in the body of the document. The example given here is role profiles, but this should be changed to whatever is relevant.

9. Document control

This should appear in most of the business analysis documentation. It sets out the revision history of the document, who needs to review or require it for information purposes and who needs to sign it off to show its contents have been agreed.

9.1. Revision history

Each time the document is distributed it should be updated with a new version number. This is to ensure all of the stakeholders are looking at the correct version and they have a summary of what has changed since they last received it. The first version is normally 0.1 and labelled as first draft. Each subsequent version should go up by 0.1 each time. When it is signed off it can be updated to version 1.

This document has had the following revisions:

Revision date	Version	Summary of changes	Author	Signed off by	Signed off date

9.2. Review/distribution

This document has been distributed to the following for review/information:

Name	Role	Date issued	Reviewer or for information	Version no.

9.3. Sign-off

By approving this document, you are confirming it complies with the documentation standards, feedback on any issues/discrepancies has been provided, and these have been adequately addressed.

Name and role or forum	Date	Supporting evidence (email/ meeting minutes)

INDEX

CPSIA information can be obtained
at www.ICGtesting.com
Printed in the USA
BVHW092241050220
571501BV00024B/1002

9 780749 497064